ENGLISH COUNTRY

OF ALL THE GREAT THINGS THAT

THE ENGLISH HAVE INVENTED AND MADE PART OF

THE CREDIT OF THE NATIONAL CHARACTER,

THE MOST PERFECT, THE MOST CHARACTERISTIC,

THE ONLY ONE THEY HAVE MASTERED

COMPLETELY IN ALL ITS DETAILS SO THAT IT

BECOMES A COMPENDIOUS ILLUSTRATION

OF THEIR SOCIAL GENIUS AND THEIR MANNERS,

IS THE WELL-APPOINTED, WELL-ADMINISTERED,

WELL-FILLED COUNTRY HOUSE.

❧ HENRY JAMES

ENGLISH

by CAROLINE SEEBOHM

and CHRISTOPHER SIMON SYKES

LIVING *in* ENGLAND'S

PRIVATE HOUSES

COUNTRY

THAMES AND HUDSON

ENDPAPER: *Taken from a fragment of wallpaper dated between 1765 and 1770.*

PREVIOUS PAGE: *Horses graze in a park in Wiltshire and detail from* Park Landscape with Sheep, *ca. 1778, watercolor by George Barret, Sr.*

Chintz, Bird and Basket, RIGHT, *designed by Geoffrey Bennison.*

Nineteenth-century block-printed wallpaper showing the influence of Italian landscape painters and detail of a stone staircase in Kent, with decorative urns, OVERLEAF.

Directory compiled by Jan Cumming
Publisher's Note: The author's acknowledgments
for permission to use materials from other sources
in this book may be found on page 286.

First published in Great Britain in 1987 by Thames and Hudson Ltd., London.
Reprinted 1988, 1994
Originally published in the United States in 1987 by Clarkson N. Potter, Inc.
201 East 50th Street, New York, New York 10022

British Library Cataloguing-in-Publication Data

A catalogue record for this book is available from the British Library

ISBN 0-500-01415-9

Manufactured in Japan
Designed by Gael Towey

ACKNOWLEDGMENTS

FIRST OF ALL, we should like to thank all the owners of the houses and gardens that appear in this book. Without their cooperation, quite simply, there would have been no book. Their generosity, interest, and hospitality were the fundamental inspiration behind these pages.

Our thanks also go to the many people on both sides of the Atlantic who helped us with information, contacts, and support, especially Gillian Saunders at the Victoria & Albert Museum, Lawrence Banks, Susan Bodo, George R. Clark, The Dowager Countess of Cranbrook, George Freeston, Victoria Glendinning, Henry Greenfield, Derek Hill, Peter Jay, Elizabeth Macfarlane, Mrs. Hilary Magnus, Michael Parkin, Tony Pell, Richard Seddon, Maggie Simmons, The Lady Trevelyan, The Hon. Kate Trevelyan.

Finally, we should like to thank our publishers, Clarkson N. Potter, Inc., especially editor-in-chief Carol Southern, who took an extraordinarily personal interest in the book and suggested many of the best ideas. We were also lucky in ensnaring Gael Towey as our art director; her exceptional talents have greatly enriched the book. We would also like to thank Ann Cahn, Judy Jacoby, and Teresa Nicholas for their skillful editorial and production work, and Amy Schuler, who took care of all the last details. As for Ann Miller, who had to coordinate endless piles of text and transparencies, as well as wrinkle out vital statistics from sources 3,000 miles apart, she deserves a medal.

CONTENTS

PREFACE

~ CAROLINE SEEBOHM

I GREW UP, not in one country house, but in four, as my father's career took him from the north to the south of England. Unlike many of the houses in this book, which have vivid, detailed histories, peopled by personalities as colorful as the times they represented, none of the four I lived in was of the slightest historical or architectural importance. It did not matter. In my recollection, they all merge into one locus of childhood, which is where we all grow up.

All my houses had roughly the same interior layout typical of every small family house. Each had a drawing room, a dining room, corridors lined with bedrooms, and, most important of all, a nursery. The nursery was our nanny's domain, and it was where we played and ate. (Like many children of the time, we were required to eat our meals with our nanny until we were 11 years old, the age presumably considered sophisticated enough to handle dining with one's parents.)

As for life indoors, it never changed. Our rooms always looked the same, even if the house was different. My parents' taste for chintz upholstery, Georgian furniture, Persian carpets, and watercolor paintings done by our relatives was to me as timeless as the grandfather clock in the hall that struck so melodiously and resolutely every hour of my childhood. Many objects and pieces of furniture my parents owned had belonged to their parents. Others they collected, and became part of the scenery. Copper luster dogs, to be searched out

in every antiques shop we visited, stared at us balefully from mantelpieces and the tops of bookshelves. Later, jugs replaced the dogs in the pottery popularity stakes, thus putting the dogs farther out of countenance. I preferred our live version, a large and very unstable black labrador, whose basket was kept under the piano. In my nightie I would huddle there beside him, hiding from my nanny who insisted that my own bed was more suitable than this canine heaven.

All our houses were attached to a particularly English landscape, whether in Yorkshire, Warwickshire, or Hertfordshire. Every Sunday after lunch my brother, my sister, and I were forced to "beat the bounds," i.e. take a brisk walk, even in the coldest weather, around our modest acres, to what end we could not imagine. It had something to do with the Victorian notion of health and, perhaps more subtly, with the idea of our making some connection to the land, however remote from the grand parks and gardens belonging to our neighbors at Castle Howard or Charlecote. I learned little about the names of flowers or trees, but I shall never forget the muddy paths along the fields, carved into trenches by tractor wheels, into which our Wellington boots happily sank, or running for the gate with an overweight bull snorting behind us, or burying dead mice caught by the local farmer's tomcat. Romantic? Hardly. Not all English country life belongs in picture books.

My first pony was a beautiful glossy creature called Flash. Every time I rode her I came home, sobbing, on foot. She threw me under trees, into ditches, over hedges. Ruthless, unsparing, Flash would find the perfect low-hanging branch and charge for it, knocking me unceremoniously into the

muddy undergrowth. My poor unversed father, so proud of this purchase for his daughter, later learned that the animal was known as The Bolter in three counties. It doesn't do to be too innocent in the country.

All this is by way of saying that while the English countryside has always evoked pictures of pastoral serenity, and given poets an endless source of inspiration ("this precious stone set in the silver sea"), yet much of English country life, like any rural existence, is a matter of making do and accepting the immutability of natural laws. One of Nancy Mitford's heroines, Linda, used to keep dead rabbits under the sofa cushions to train her hunting dog. This down-to-earth approach, while offensive to the squeamish, recognizes the relationship between society and nature, and promotes a sense of perspective. What is perhaps unique about England is its assumption of stability—hence my enduring images of home.

Detail of A Summer Day, *ca. 1832, watercolor by John Sell Cotman.*

PREFACE

THE STRONGEST MEMORY I hold of Sledmere, the Yorkshire house in which I was brought up, is that it was always full of people. To begin with the family, including our parents, numbered eight. Then there was a large household staff, all of whom lived in, consisting of the butler, two footmen, a pantryboy, a pantrymaid, the cook, a scullery-boy, the housekeeper, the nanny, a nursemaid, the secretary, and a French governess, as well as an army of dailies; all this before the arrival of the, literally, hundreds of friends who came to visit my parents throughout the year to indulge in what appeared to be an endless round of country pursuits. They came for the races at York and Doncaster, for the shooting and the hunting, the tennis and the croquet, for Christmas and Easter, high days and holidays, filling the house with their chatter and laughter, the distant hum of which would float up nightly to our bedrooms on the nursery floor. No matter how many guests were staying, the kitchens could always cope, for the estate was completely self-sufficient. Each morning the dairyman would bring fresh milk and butter, the gardeners would deliver fruit and vegetables, and one of the gamekeepers or the butcher would arrive with game or meat. Never for a moment did this frenetic existence cease, and Sledmere was perfectly suited for it, having been built in 1760 to support an 18th-century way of life.

The house was a children's paradise, and when our parents were away we ran wild in it. There were long corridors to run up and down, stone

floors to tricycle and bicycle upon, acres of polished wood across which to slide, countless rooms for games of hide-and-seek, and spooky attics and cellars to explore. We would await our parents' return with some trepidation, for there was invariably some mischief to be accounted for, such as the breakage of yet another valuable vase (they seemed to be everywhere, acting as doorstops, walking-stick holders, water bowls for the dogs, etc.) or an attempt to set fire to a hayloft on the farm. Their arrival also meant banishment back up to the top floor of the house, where the nursery, night nursery, and schoolroom were. This was where we slept, did our lessons, took our meals, and generally lived out our lives. Only at teatime were we allowed a foray into that hallowed adult world, when we were dressed up in our best little shorts, shirts, and frocks, brought down to see our parents, and shown off to whatever visitor happened to be present. It was an incredibly ordered, secure, and privileged existence, so far removed from my life today that it might have taken place in another century.

My eldest brother now lives at Sledmere in quite a different way from that of our parents, looked after by a cook and butler and one or two dailies. Like many other country house owners, financial necessity has obliged him to open Sledmere to the public and he has moved into a sitting room and library converted out of two bedrooms. Fresh produce still arrives each morning, though in smaller quantities, but at times such as Christmas, or for a big shoot, when twenty people sit down for lunch, Sledmere still experiences echoes of its past.

Pink roses, FAR LEFT, *on a summer day.*
Blue roses, chintz, LEFT, *designed by Geoffrey Bennison.*
Engraving of Biddesden House by R. Stone, OVERLEAF.

INTRODUCTION

ASK A CHILD to draw a house, and what do we see? A square or rectangular box, with a hipped roof, chimney, symmetrical doors and windows, and maybe a path with flowers and a surrounding fence. This innocent picture is an almost exact prototype of the English country house. In its developed form —a freestanding house with classical proportions set in a country landscape—it expresses our most fundamental idea of home.

This image should not be confused with the great English stately homes—Hardwick, Blenheim, Wilton, Knole, Longleat—which continue to summon up visions of splendor in the tourist's mind. These grand buildings are no more houses in the domestic sense of the word than is the White House in Washington. They are museums, amusement parks, obsolete political symbols, monuments to the past. Filled with treasures acquired during Britain's long imperial history, their gift to the present is only nostalgia, a whiff of champagne-laden dust.

But the observant traveler along the country roads of England cannot fail to observe indications of the existence of a number of splendid houses without National Trust signs, public markers indicating "House Open Today," or other such institutional directions. A fine pair of gates here, a handsome park there, a long low wall—these are clues that, if pursued, reveal a different view of English country life. Smaller, perhaps, and more practical than the ornate mansions dedicated to personal glory, these houses are as exquisite in design, proportion, and geographical situation as any to be found in the guidebooks. It is to these houses that we hope to divert the attention until now devoted exclusively to their richer and more public cousins.

The houses celebrated in this book belong to the land in the way that English country houses have always belonged to the land, with horses, dogs, cows, sheep, and hens as essential accessories to the landscape. They have been handed down in many cases through several generations of the same family, and their interiors demonstrate the kind of warmth and mellowness that springs from generational care.

"The house stamps its own character on all ways of living: I am ruled by a continuity that I cannot see," wrote Elizabeth Bowen about her beloved Bowen's Court. Built occasionally in hopes of royal favors or for public approbation, but always for personal satisfaction, such houses are today sometimes working farms, sometimes the focal point of a village, sometimes the last remnant of a feudal society. But in all cases they have a beauty and timelessness that have come to represent an ideal to architects and designers all over the world.

We want to take the reader, like a benign voyeur, through those discreet gates and into those graceful parks, behind the protective walls of these manors, rectories, and farmhouses. (Cottages are excluded. Defined by the dictionary as a "small, humble dwelling"—though many, of course, are not—the cottage represents a different aspect of country life, both in its more modest social context and in its modern role as suburban escape.) Of the houses whose interiors are represented here, none is a National Trust property; all are privately owned. Only three—Doddington Hall, Deene Park, and Sledmere House—are open to the public. The rest are private, secluded from the curious outsider, little pockets of civilization in an increasingly wild world —living examples of the English country ideal.

INTO MY HEART AN AIR THAT KILLS
FROM YON FAR COUNTRY BLOWS.
WHAT ARE THOSE BLUE REMEMBERED HILLS,
WHAT SPIRES, WHAT FARMS ARE THOSE?
— A. E. HOUSMAN

The

LAND

IN ANGLO-SAXON ENGLAND, as in much of Europe after the Dark Ages, most land belonged to the king, who, in return for allegiance and practical support, granted parcels of it to his nobles. (The titles came later.) These estates, never large enough to threaten the king's power, were then subdivided or rented to bailiffs and vassals, creating small communities of peasants, livestock, and equipment—the hub of the feudal manor.

The word *manor* comes from the Latin *maneo*, meaning "I remain" or "I dwell." The manor was the estate of the landowning noble, or lord, on whom the community depended for its livelihood. (*Lord* is an abbreviation of the Anglo-Saxon word *hlaford*, which means one who provides *hlaf*, or a loaf of bread.) One of the first tasks every English schoolchild must undertake is a drawing of a feudal manor, with its hall (house), church, mill, village, fields, barns, and boundaries. For 500 years, the relationship between a house and its land has been reinforced in the English consciousness alongside the letters of the alphabet. (In current cockney slang, "Get off my manor" means "Get off my turf.")

When William the Conqueror, with the help of his Norman armies, acquired England in 1066, he brought with him certain innovations. One was that from then on, all land belonged to the king—the first act of nationalization in England's history. To this end, he ordered the compilation of the *Domesday Book* in 1086.

"The King had muckle thought and deep speech with his wise-men about this land, how it was set, and with what men. Then he sent his men all over England into each shire and let them find out how many hundred hides were in that shire, and what the King had himself of land or cattle in those lands. . . ."

An autumn landscape, PREVIOUS PAGE *—the flat, rolling countryside of Yorkshire, one of England's northernmost counties. Detail of* The Shepherd: Evening, Buckinghamshire, 1845, *watercolor by Francis Oliver Finch (1802–1862).*

Cows grazing, RIGHT, *in a Yorkshire pasture.*

The extensive acreage of England's northern counties escaped the Enclosure Acts, which divided land into parcels by Parliamentary decree during the 18th and 19th centuries.

Since all land belonged to the king, land could not be owned by an individual. The individual instead had rights to land, and if he accumulated enough rights it was tantamount to freehold ownership. (In continental Europe, the Roman conception of *dominium* was preferred, which meant that one could by law own the actual, real earth beneath one's feet.)

These rights could be passed on from proprietor to heir by means of a legal binder or by the terms of a will. The law of primogeniture, whereby the firstborn son automatically inherits his father's title and property, was another innovation introduced to the English by the Normans, who had a healthy respect for the smooth succession of manorial powers from one generation to the next. (Females were not considered up to the role.) It could happen, however, that the lord had no son, indeed no children at all. In order to continue to keep his land within the family, a further law was created in the 14th century that allowed landowners to "entail" their land, that is, to place a restriction on it in perpetuity. The preferred restriction for the English was to allow the inheritance of land only through the male line. (That is why Vita Sackville-West could not inherit Knole.)

The application of these two land laws has been responsible for more family troubles than any other social taboo except, perhaps, incest. No wonder so many second sons of landed gentry took to wine, women, and a life abroad. Yet the land laws also guaranteed a stability of land ownership equal only to the dynastic successions of ancient China. Although the power of the manorial lords changed over the centuries, and new classes of property owners (yeomen, and then parvenu businessmen) emerged from the breakdown of the feudal system, as long as English law allowed a landowner to dispose of his property in any way he wished by deed during his life or by last will and testament, his land could survive intact after his death. Although primogeniture in England today applies only to a hereditary title that automatically passes to the eldest son on the death of his father (the firstborn son only gets the land automatically if it is entailed), the custom remains embedded in many an English testator's mind.

How different from France's property laws, which, in spite of providing such an inspired model, were totally altered by the Code Napoléon (applying also to Holland and Belgium). Today, when a French landowner dies, the major portion of his property descends by legal right to his children, the division regulated by law in equal portions regardless of sex. De Tocqueville was quick to note the contrasting effect of these two laws on the countries concerned: "Framed in one way," he pointed out, "the law of succession combines and concentrates property and power in a few hands; it causes a landed aristocracy to flourish." In countries where the legislature has established an equal division of the spoils, on the other hand, property, and particularly landed property, must have a permanent tendency to decrease—"rapidly dispersing families and fortunes."

England being a small country, the limits to a man's land were carefully defined. In medieval times, the manorial boundaries were clearly marked, but beyond them were open fields, privately owned but farmed in common by smallholders and peasants. As early as the 15th century, such fields were beginning to be enclosed, to graze sheep or sow crops. As the population increased, forests were cut down to make more land (hence the profusion of wood used in Tudor architecture), and wild pasture tamed, for both aristocratic landowners and the rising middle-class yeomen.

In 1692, a land tax was imposed by William III to pay for his wars with the French, which further threatened the small farmer, who could not afford to pay it and

Sheep near a stream in Wiltshire, ABOVE, *horses in a Norfolk park,* BELOW.

A *view of 10 counties*, ABOVE, *from Hergest Ridge: Carmarthen, Shropshire, Radnorshire, Worcestershire, Montgomeryshire, Gloucestershire, Monmouthshire, Breconshire, Cardiganshire, and Herefordshire.*

The countryside in Northamptonshire, RIGHT, *called by Sir George Sitwell "the heart of England." Like most of the country, it is divided by 500 years of the Enclosure Acts into neat squares.*

That famous deer poacher, William Shakespeare, would have been sorely tempted by this herd in Norfolk, BELOW.

On Hergest Ridge overlooking Herefordshire and the Welsh Marches, OVERLEAF.

was forced to sell to the rich barons who already owned sizable estates. The death blow to the open fields policy and the smallholder came with the agricultural revolution of the 18th century, when new plows, threshing machines, and other equipment, plus the introduction of new crops such as turnips, swedes, and potatoes, made farming a sophisticated financial proposition. A series of Acts of Parliament between 1750 and 1850 systematically enclosed most of the still available land and produced instead a geometric landscape divided by hedges.

As the peasant-farmer was excluded from the field enclosure movement, so was he unable to take advantage of the decline of feudalism. As the feudal manors evolved into newer, grander estates, it was not the peasants who benefited from the extended property, needless to say, because it had already been cleverly entailed by the legal advisers of the powerful land barons. (Dickens wrote a whole novel, *Bleak House,* to highlight the appalling injustices of English real property law.) A national survey carried out in 1873 revealed that 40 percent of all the land in England and Wales was owned by no more than 1,700 landowners. (Even in prerevolutionary France, the French nobility never owned much more than 40 percent of the countryside; the rest belonged to the Church and the peasantry.) A list of some of the holdings before World War I is quite astonishing—the Ickworth estate, for instance, consisted of approximately 30,000 acres in West Suffolk, 12,000 in East Suffolk, 20,000 in Lincolnshire, and 800 in Essex.

Owing to increasingly restrictive inheritance taxes imposed by successive Labor governments, such huge figures have been greatly whittled down. Moreover, estate owners today must struggle to afford the enormous staff

required to keep up their acreage. But very few country houses today come without some "country." While heirs to large estates have been forced, by crippling death duties, to sell off land, the dream of owning one's own estate remains constant. Throughout the centuries, the goal of the *nouveaux riches* has always been to see their children live "as to the manor born."

Even Benjamin Disraeli, that maverick political genius of the late 19th century, fell for the mystique. He acquired Hughenden, in Buckinghamshire, a wonderful manor house dating from before the Norman Conquest, in hopes that this might make him more acceptable to his peers. It is an indication of his pride in the elevation that on his tombstone he had inscribed, "Lord of this Manor." (Hughenden, now owned by the National Trust, is within walking distance of the more famous Chequers, the prime minister's country residence, another manor house dating from King John's time.)

The enduring nature of English feudal history is most convincingly proved by the existence, even today, of deeds attached to manorial land that entitle the owner to call himself a "lord." These titles, many dating from before the Norman Conquest, are documents that have never been invalidated, although the land has been sold and divided many times. Whoever owns one assumes the duties of a feudal lord, and is granted, according to the manorial deed, certain rights conferred by royal charter. Real estate agents are now recovering these titles and selling them for up to $15,000. Some surprised house buyers are discovering that their house comes with a bonus of manorial title and rights, and some even more surprised landowners are discovering that someone else has manorial rights. Gerald R. Rand, 24th Lord of the Manor of Lynford, a 100-room house in Norfolk, is suing the present landowners of part of his manorial title for £180,000, which he contends is royalty rights due on a gravel pit. The feudal spirit lives.

The P R O

WELL! SOME PEOPLE TALK OF MORALITY,
AND SOME OF RELIGION,
BUT GIVE ME A LITTLE SNUG PROPERTY.
MARIA EDGEWORTH
1767–1849

P E R T Y

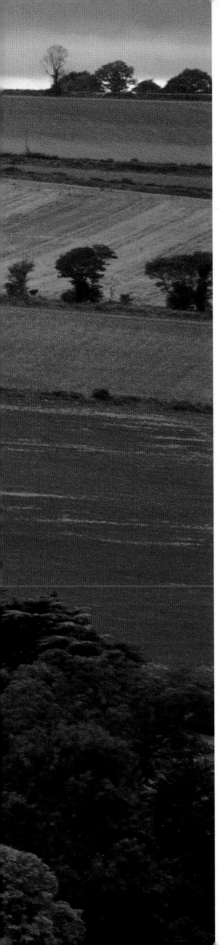

ALONG WITH THE traditional importance attached to the ownership of land comes another notion—that of privacy. An Englishman's home may be his castle, but he prefers his battlements secluded from the curious stares of the general public. Large parks, a string of wheat fields, a winding driveway lined by oaks or poplars, not only indicate a certain position in the world but also ensure obscurity from the passing tourist. Add to this the aesthetic quality inherent in the subtle buildup of suspense, the elegant suspension of vista, that a long driveway provides, and you are encountering one of the prime experiences of the country house visitor.

Most driveways meander through considerable parkland, where sheep, cows, or horses graze. Many drives have cattle grids—rows of bars spaced so wide that an animal's foot may not gain purchase. The sound of a car crossing the grid, a deep metallic rattle, is one that evokes the English countryside as powerfully as a pheromone.

The gates of a house are often the only indication of its presence. One must find one's way by judicious spotting of a fence, a gravel path, a large pair of pillars, some unusual stonework. (How unlike America, where the ubiquitous flag-waving mailbox by the side of the road, often in clusters like a dovecote, announces in large letters, for all the world to see, the name of who lives there.)

Walls may mark the limits of property, but they are not, as in the Chinese tradition, an essential element to an English country house's layout. Some manor

The village of Poyntington, in Dorset, LEFT *and* ABOVE, *manorial in form with 14th-century church and on its left, from the same date, the courthouse. In this place during the "Bloody Assizes" of 1685, the infamous Lord Chief Justice Jeffreys sentenced to brutal deaths the supporters of the Protestant rebel Duke of Monmouth, who had attempted to remove his Catholic uncle, James II, from the throne.*

Oast-houses for storing hops, LEFT, *are typical sights in Kent.*

A dramatic line of poplars, PREVIOUS PAGE, *leading to Heale House, near Salisbury, in Wiltshire; and a detail of Bromley Hill, watercolor by Peter de Wint (1784–1849).*

houses, by definition, are situated close to a village, their feudal roots. These houses often have protective walls to separate them from the outside world. Rectories are obviously connected to the churches to which they are (or were) attached, and frequently have walled gardens to maintain privacy from a prying flock. Kitchen gardens are almost always surrounded by good high walls, as protection from weather and also, perhaps, local pilfering. (If the house is of a certain size, it may boast a lodge at the gates, a tiny version of the main house, from which the gatekeeper keeps guard over uninvited guests or animals. But lodges generally come with larger houses than those discussed here.)

The desire for privacy seems somehow at odds with the idea of the English country house as social magnet, as venue for amusing weekends among the rich and

R*ich farming country,* ABOVE, *surrounds Sledmere House, in Yorkshire, where members of the Sykes family have lived since the middle of the 18th century.* RIGHT, *Sledmere in winter.*

A *typical hedge-lined country lane,* LEFT. *Driving may be perilous but it is considered cowardly to use one's horn.*

famous. But while the bigger houses, and certainly the stately homes, were built to announce to the world a man's status, wealth, and position in society, the smaller manor houses served a much more modest function. Many evolved from feudal traditions, and therefore remained committed to the working of the land rather than to the working of a room. Others were built as genuine retreats, places to hide in after a busy season in London, easy-to-run houses where only a handful of servants would be required. Hunting lodges, which date from the 16th century, filled a need for sportsmen who wanted a simple country camp, and "follies," or eye-catchers, became chic rendezvous by the end of the 18th century for sport of all kinds. Those that remain continue to exert their charms over 20th-century urban escapists.

A *well-built wall and Gothic archway,* ABOVE *and* LEFT, *dating from the 1800s, part of the outbuildings of a house in Herefordshire.*

Graceful *18th-century wrought-iron gates,* RIGHT, *make a fine entrance to a country house on the Hampshire border.*

Feudal *relations,* ABOVE RIGHT: *the village church looks over the walled garden of a small manor house in Wiltshire.*

A *16th-century doorway in Kent,* FAR RIGHT. *To enter, the visitor is required to step over a generous clump of parsley blooming on the threshold.*

The Convent in the Woods,
Stourton, Wiltshire,
OVERLEAF, *a small Gothic
folly built about 1765 by
Sir Henry Hoare, the landscape
architect responsible for the
famous gardens at nearby
Stourhead. Sir Henry was an
ardent admirer of the rustic
and the irregular, as can
be seen in the stonework of the
arched entrance to the folly
—a brave contrast to the Palladian style aspired to by most
others in the 18th century.*

The H O

A COMFORTABLE HOUSE IS A GREAT
SOURCE OF HAPPINESS.
IT RANKS IMMEDIATELY AFTER HEALTH
AND A GOOD CONSCIENCE.
— REV. SYDNEY SMITH
1771–1845

U S E S

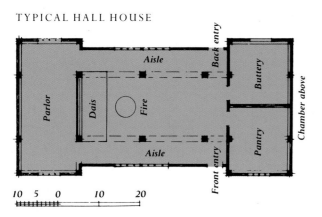

TYPICAL HALL HOUSE

Parlor | Dais | Fire | Aisle | Back entry | Buttery | Chamber above

Aisle | Front entry | Pantry

10 5 0 10 20

Blo' Norton Hall, an Elizabethan manor in Norfolk, dated 1585, with typical half-timbering and high chimneys of the period. The other side, BOTTOM, shows the Elizabethan E-shaped house in embryo—the two gables, with decorative step-style brickwork, flanking the core medieval rectangular hall. Floor plan, BELOW, of a characteristic medieval hall. The Normans introduced aisles to the basic Anglo-Saxon rectangular layout.

DESIGN HISTORIANS TEND to date English architectural history from the Norman invasion, but the English lived in houses long before 1066. Earliest remains show influence of the country's Roman masters —brick walls, frescoes, heating ducts, courtyards, mosaics. Almost all these have disappeared, leaving the field to the Dark Age inhabitants, who reverted to more primitive styles—stone igloos, or wattle-and-daub huts, with thatch and the occasional timber framing. The Anglo-Saxons who emerged as leaders from this period failed to capitalize on the house-building potential and have left few examples of architectural innovation.

William the Conqueror rewarded his Norman army with large estates on the small defeated island. Many of the newly created barons and bishops showed their gratitude by building lavish cathedrals to God and fortified castles for self-defense. As the country settled down and fear of war diminished, the castles were abandoned in favor of more open, informal dwellings, and domestic architecture really began to flourish.

The timber-framed medieval manor was simply a communal dosshouse for the feudal lord and his employees, who ate and slept in a long central hall (hence the rectangular shape of most early English houses). This overworked space was ventilated by the hole in the roof above the open hearth, and by windows—or more correctly, "wind-eyes"—in the form of vertical slits, which may have prevented the random arrow from reaching its mark, but were also just the right shape to attract the most horrendous drafts. (Glass, a very expensive commodity, was not in general use until the 18th century.) Originally one story, two stories had been added to most houses by the 13th century.

During this period, wall fireplaces replaced the open hearth, but the chimney flue was still an impractical duct up the wall through the roof. By the 17th century, brick chimneys had been invented, giving more flexibility to the placement of the fireplace, and this development, combined with an increasing sense of hierarchy, drove the grander manorial lords out of the hall and into the "great chamber," which moved upstairs and became part of a private suite, where audiences were given. People wanted privacy. The bower became the parlor

Elizabethan architecture at its zenith, RIGHT, *Chastleton House, in Oxfordshire, built in 1603, its vigorous sequence of bays and gables providing a dramatic vista of perspective and scale.*

Sledmere House, PAGES 22– 23, *built during the "golden age" of English country houses in the 18th century. The parkland was laid out by Lancelot "Capability" Brown, whose most complete landscape can be seen at Blenheim Palace. Also, a detail of* Purley Hall, Berkshire, *watercolor by Francis Cotes (1726–1770).*

(from the French *parler,* to talk), and a buttery and pantry were added to the ground floor. (Most of the words that began to form a language of interior decorating—chamber, ceiling, tapestry, cushion, chair, for instance—came from Norman French, the language of the upper classes.) Thus the hall lost its function as command module of the manor, and instead became the conduit, by means of an impressive central staircase, up to the first floor. Only the name lingered, attached to countless houses—Blickling Hall, Haddon Hall —to remind us of its former importance.

The Elizabethans created a building boom, adapting Renaissance designs and adding to them their own ideas of style, employing European architects and craftsmen as well as producing fine homegrown ones, such as John Thorpe, an expert in Palladian design, considered England's first Palladian architect, and Robert Smythson, Queen Elizabeth's master mason, who designed Longleat House in Wiltshire, Hardwick Hall in Derbyshire, and Wollaton Hall in Nottinghamshire. Some of the best houses in the country date from the late 16th and early 17th centuries, when wealthy landowners vied with their neighbors in building bigger and better mansions for themselves. Queen Elizabeth I only fueled the competition. She was a

Castle Farm, Sledmere, ABOVE AND BELOW, *an 18th-century folly built to please the eye of the residents looking out of the windows of the big house a short distance away. A working farm until very recently, the folly is now lived in by Christopher Simon Sykes and his family.*

keen traveler and liked to check on her subjects in their own houses—at great cost to the householder, needless to say. (Architectural historian Mark Girouard suggests that she did this on purpose in order to get certain overambitious subjects into such financial difficulties "that the sting was taken out of them.") It is certainly true that during the 17th century several houses were built solely in hopes of attracting the Queen to stay. (Almost every country house in England, it seems, claims to have a bed in which Queen Elizabeth slept.)

The Elizabethans were enchanted by glass, and their exuberant use of windows, with bays and gables, confirms the pleasure architects and builders derived from this new and exciting material. Windows became so much in demand that some clever advisers of William and Mary introduced, in 1697, a tax upon windows (just like that upon chintz). Houses with more than six windows had to pay a sum which increased several times during the next one hundred years—that is why one still sees many Georgian houses in England with windows blocked up or painted in trompe l'oeil manner. (One could write a book on the influence of crown taxes upon the development of English decoration.)

While Inigo Jones (1573–1652) is regarded by many as England's greatest architect (a keen Palladian, his most famous building is Wilton House in Wiltshire), to many people's taste, the most perfect English country houses are the 18th-century ones, their qualities deriving from the much-admired period in English history during the successful reigns of Queen Anne and the first three King Georges, when artistic talent abounded and country virtues prospered. Under the influence of Jones and his followers, John Webb, Hugh May, and Christopher Wren, the classical orders and harmony prevailed.

Lord David Cecil refers to them in his book on Jane Austen, herself the perfect chronicler of that golden age: "Graceful and mannerly," he salutes the houses,

"with their well-proportioned exteriors of grey stone or rosy brick, their white-painted woodwork, their sunny sitting rooms small or spacious, their bedrooms gay with striped wallpaper and flowered chintz; while interior and exterior alike are dignified by an unobtrusive unfailing sense of style."

Heale House, a 17th-century manor with exquisite gardens, where King Charles II briefly hid following his defeat by Cromwell at the Battle of Worcester in 1651, before fleeing to exile in France.

By the 19th century the hall had staged a comeback. Since the major entertaining rooms by that time had moved back down to the ground floor again (the story of English architecture has always contained an element of musical chairs), there was no need for the staircase to dominate the hall. Moreover, architects and designers saw it was necessary to re-create one aspect of the hall's medieval role—as a central greeting place—now for guests rather than vassals, also as a way station for servants, and

A farmhouse in Cornwall, full of history. Formerly a monastery, it reaches even farther into the past, thanks to the discovery in the garden of a skeleton buried in the fetal position as was the custom during the Dark Ages.

as entrance to the drawing room, dining room, and other reception rooms. (The origin of "withdrawing room" is believed to stem from King Charles II's custom of asking visitors to wait for him in a room adjacent to his bed-chamber, in which he generally held audience. For more on Charles II, the Karl Lagerfeld of his day, see the next chapter.)

As the Victorian idea of the country-house week-end took hold, and people flocked to the country for entertainment, the houses were required to function in another role. This time room had to be found, not only for the fleets of servants who ran the household, but also for the staff of visiting nobility. ("When my mother was a girl," wrote Lady Mary Clive in 1964, "if anyone wished to have her to stay they were forced to put up five people—herself, father, mother, maid and valet.") An added complication was that Victorians preferred their servants to be invisible at all times. This meant the introduction of "backstairs," with a rabbit warren of little bedrooms upstairs, and kitchen, pantry, scullery, and so forth downstairs, behind a green baize door (to muffle menial noise), separating the higher from the lower orders. Most of the latter part of the 20th century has been taken up by house owners undoing what the Victorians wrought, tearing down wings, abolishing servants' quarters, demolishing ball-rooms, and so on.

London still empties at weekends like American cities in the summertime. Events of the social season still attract the kind of house parties that took place in the last century. Major race meetings such as Goodwood and Ascot, Badminton and other sporting events (see Directory), still pack the country houses as in the old days. But few are the maids, butlers, valets, and cooks. Gone are the ball-rooms and servants' wings. The small country house has reverted to its 18th-century ideal.

Seend Green House in Melksham, Wiltshire, dating from 1620, with Georgian additions made by the Duke of Somerset for his sister in 1760.

FOR THERE IS A MUSIC
WHEREVER THERE IS A HARMONY,
ORDER OR PROPORTION.
SIR THOMAS BROWNE
1605–1682

T h e R

O O M S

SOCIETY, FRIENDSHIP AND LOVE

DIVINELY BESTOW'D UPON MAN.

⤙ WILLIAM COWPER

1731–1800

MEETING

The wonderfully busy hall at Bereleigh, RIGHT, *a farmhouse in Hampshire. Dating from 1600, it seems almost medieval in function. The main entrance of the house, it is also both study and sitting room. By the captain's desk are racks for whips and hunting horns. The carved ceiling and fine moldings indicate its authentic Tudor origins. A cozy corner,* ABOVE, *in a Yorkshire manor house, with family memorabilia.*

A *corner of the ballroom,* PREVIOUS PAGE, *in Seend Green House in Wiltshire. The graceful Gothic windows and carved ceiling are of classic Georgian design. Also, a detail of* Interior, *watercolor by Adrian Hill.*

THE DUTCH HUMANIST Erasmus, who visited England between 1509 and 1513, was less than 100 percent impressed with the first English Country House Look: "The floors are commonly of clay, strewed with rushes, under which lies unmolested an ancient collection of beer, spittle, excrement of dogs and cats and everything that is nasty."

The interior evolution of the smaller English country houses moved only gradually out of this somewhat basic decorating style, thanks largely to a desire for self-aggrandizement, a love of comfort, and a talent for acquisitiveness. Until the 17th century, furniture and upholstery were regarded as secondary to the building, and although often rich in carving and tapestries, interiors developed without much attention to detail.

King Charles II changed all that. Escaping to France after his father, King Charles I, was beheaded in 1649 during the political and religious war between what

were known as the Cavaliers (Royalists) and Roundheads (Republicans), the unthroned monarch spent a very useful part of his exile at the court of Louis XIV, where he learned how sophisticated life was lived. (It would be difficult adequately to estimate the cultural influence of the French on English life, from Gothic architecture, property law, social behavior, and language to the visual arts and gardening.) On his triumphant return as king in 1660, he quickly saw that his countrymen lagged far behind in ideas about interior decorating, and in consequence craftsmen from France and the Low Countries were imported to impart their skills to the backward English. Gateleg tables, spiral-turned chairs, embroidered upholstery, veneering, marquetry, carved frames, ceramics, and other decorative techniques all made their appearance, largely thanks to the Sun King's brilliant court, during the Stuart years of the late 17th century. (Thanks also to Louis XIV's misguided expulsion of the Huguenots in 1685, many skilled French *ébénistes* fled to England permanently.)

By the 18th century, known as the "golden age" of the English country house, it was customary to allow your architect to do the interior decorating if he so wished. William Kent, the Chippendale family, and Robert Adam, for instance, took an immense interest in the insides of their houses. Kent interiors are rich in stucco work, painted decoration, and marble, with elaborately carved furniture, gilt swags, shell motifs, and festoons. He was the first to believe in personally controlling the selection of every detail of an interior, from tassels to door handles. Thomas Chippendale was the son of a Yorkshire carpenter, and his (mostly mahogany) furniture in the Rococo style, including Neo-Gothic and Chinoiserie, is still famous today. Robert Adam created a style that dominated England and France

A *country drawing room,* BELOW, *with an 18th-century French rug, William Morris fabric for the upholstery, and dried grasses in the fireplace.*

An *informal sitting room,* RIGHT, *striking for its remarkable display of pictures, a family collection. The chintz-covered slipper chair, old marble fireplace, and warm walls create an inviting atmosphere.*

Fine Chinese furniture brings a trace of formality to this drawing room of Hartridge Manor Farm in Kent. The slipcovers are cotton and the curtain fabric is a famous William Morris willow pattern. The Hartridge family, who lived here in the 17th century, emigrated to America for religious reasons.

throughout the century, of delicate, highly embroidered neoclassical designs in furniture, urns, plasterwork, and wall decoration. He liked to match a carpet design with a ceiling design, for instance, creating a classical harmony.

These artists were expensive, and could only be afforded by very rich patrons. It was not until the 19th century that designer and thinker William Morris persuaded his followers not only that the interior arts should be as important as the exterior, but that they should be accessible to everybody. Morris's own contribution to this credo, in the form of furniture, textiles, wallpapers, and glass, gave the bourgeoisie an outlet that can still be seen in houses across the country.

Where the English excelled was in acquiring things —loot, if you will—from the countries they visited and sometimes conquered. As the wealth of the landowners increased, so did their acquisitiveness, and galleries and cabinets were set aside for treasures brought back from around the world. As the British Empire stretched its tentacles farther and farther eastward, the size and quality of these collections grew. Greek, Egyptian, Italian, French,

Chinese, and Indian sculpture, furniture, glass, porcelain, and paintings soon became as English in manner as the owners who acquired them. No wonder gossip (untrue) had it that the Duke of Wellington, after defeating Napoleon at Waterloo, was "spending his nights unhooking pictures from the walls of the Louvre," as Susan Mary Alsop reveals in *The Congress Dances.*

You might have beautiful treasures, but you did not flaunt them. It was considered the height of vulgarity to show off one's riches, thus valuable paintings and objects were treated with less reverence than today's investment-conscious collectors would ever dream of. "If it was a lovely house with lovely things in it," Lady Marjorie Stirling remembers,

"some hosts and hostesses, if they thought you were interested, took immense pleasure in showing you round them, which I liked. But it was considered bad form to remark on people's possessions; uninvited, it was very rude to say how marvellous they were. At my first dinner party, I think, to which I went with my parents, I did the most

A *more formal drawing room, with Ionic columns, a fine 18th-century stone-carved fireplace, silk and linen slipcovers, a tapestry hanging behind the Chinese cabinet, and horse paintings in the style of George Stubbs.*

appalling thing. A simply beautiful china plate was put down in front of me, and I turned the plate up to see what it was. I got the most frightful row from my mother afterwards."

Lady Marjorie might be cheered by the story of the man who admired some Chippendale chairs belonging to the present Lord Derby's grandfather. Said his lordship, "Damn cheek, that fella noticing my chairs."

This casual attitude was reversed when American decorators such as Elsie de Wolfe, Rose Cumming, Ruby Ross Wood, Eleanor S. Brown, and Dorothy Draper began scouring the world for paintings, furniture, and textiles to bring back to their rich clients' new mansions at the beginning of this century. Americans really invented the modern idea of the interior decorator, and their admiration of the English style helped raise the consciousness of house owners at home. The grande dame of American decorating since the twenties, Mrs. Henry Parish II, brought chintz, petit-point, animal paintings, and other paraphernalia of the English country house into the grand mansions of the American rich, and they loved it.

The English were slow to appreciate decoration as a profession, but a few 20th-century decorators working in England, such as Syrie Maugham, Sybil Colefax, and Nancy Lancaster, and the distinguished historian and restorer John Fowler, drew people's attention to the historical value of the decorative arts, particularly with respect to preserving the country's rapidly eroding collections. The decorating firm Colefax and Fowler became a repository of this knowledge. Nancy Lancaster, John Fowler's second partner, is an American, and yet she seems to have known instinctively how to create what has become known as the English Country House Look. As John Cornforth points out in his book *Inspiration of the Past,* Mrs. Lancaster was a Langhorne, whose home was in Virginia, perhaps the place closest to England in its culture and style of living. She

always loved the old Virginia houses "in mellow decline after the Civil War," and brought with her this sense of understated beauty when she moved to England in the late twenties. The two houses, Kelmarsh and Ditchley, where she lived with her second husband, Ronald Tree, were models of unaffected taste and comfort.

In spite of these few talented efforts, most of the English, from the Royal Family on down, firmly continue to disavow the idea of any house looking "decorated." The wise Nancy Lancaster intentionally faded her chintzes, fatigued her furniture, and cut out the frills, ensuring her a permanent place in the hearts of her adopted countrymen.

There is, however, a serenity to the English country interior; well-stuffed furniture, muted colors, family mementos, flowers bunched heedlessly into vases, a pleasing air of informality, even in the grander drawing rooms. This sense of well-being is the result of a social system that has managed to sustain its structure and traditions for over 900 years. No other country in Europe can claim such a record of unbroken enjoyment in country pleasures, and the rooms perfectly express this. Revolutions, pestilence, earthquakes, acts of God, have left the Englishman undisturbed in his private heaven.

For decorative arts devotees, social stability and an aversion to the idea of decoration must be regarded as limitations. But within these admitted confines, every room pictured here expresses a remarkable individuality. It is on the details that the eye must linger—a pile of books, a wall of pictures, a mantelpiece, a desk—for each tells a story as unique as may be found in any contemporary anthology. It is these details that give the rooms their hospitable look and provide the air of relaxed elegance that is the envy of imitators.

A stripped-down look focuses attention on the Gothic architecture of Sir Henry Hoare's folly in the Wiltshire woods, achieved with furniture airily arranged and draped in cotton spreads.

He May live WITHOUT BOOKS,

WHAT IS KNOWLEDGE BUT GRIEVING?

HE MAY LIVE WITHOUT HOPE,

WHAT IS HOPE BUT DECEIVING?

HE MAY LIVE WITHOUT LOVE,

WHAT IS PASSION BUT PINING?

BUT WHERE IS THE MAN THAT CAN

LIVE WITHOUT DINING?

❧ ROBERT BULWER, EARL OF LYTTON

E A T I N G

AT ABOUT THE END of the 16th century, the feudal lords came to the conclusion that rather than go on observing their vassals gnawing on chicken legs day after day, they would rather eat with people of their own class, and the dining room was born. It had different names—great chamber in the early 17th century, saloon in the late 17th and early 18th centuries. The first recognized dining room was probably at Houghton Hall, Norfolk. It was designed for Sir Robert Walpole by William Kent in about 1731. Entertaining had become yet another way of demonstrating to the world how rich, powerful, and exclusive you were, and a special room, designated specifically for dining, was included on all the best floor plans. They grew ever bigger and grander, to reflect their owners' status. They always had two doors —one for the gentry, one for the servants. Servants were required to become increasingly invisible. In one large mansion in Suffolk, the gardeners were instructed

The dining room at Aske Hall, Yorkshire. Its simple aspect is enriched by the fine portraits and an elaborately carved fireplace.

40

Late-20th-century dining—an intimate space with room for four or six, BELOW. *Artist James Reeve's dining area is filled with his unusual collections, including a snakeskin and a Spanish 18th-century figure of Jesus. A rich quilt tablecloth reminds the visitor of the atmospheric room's country setting.*

Artist's kitchen, RIGHT, *opposite the dining area. The glowing golden wall color is achieved by dabbing raw siena onto white water-based paint. The table is scrubbed pine, with unmatched 18th- and 19th-century chairs.*

to hide behind hedges if the lord or lady of the house happened to stroll by.

The room's square footage had continually to be enlarged, to encompass the increasingly elaborate formal evening dress of the 18th and 19th centuries, and to allow footmen to pass between each chair to deliver the food and wine. (According to her personal maid, Lady Astor liked to squeeze everybody close together, because it made for a better party. This caused much displeasure, not only to her footmen, but also to Winston Churchill, who on one occasion sat through the whole dinner without eating, and at the end remarked, "Thirty dishes served and no damn room to eat one.")

"For a big dinner party, a really posh dinner party," recalls Patricia, Viscountess Hambleden, of the days before World War I, "you would have either thick or clear soup, followed by fish, followed by the entrée—chicken or quails. Then you had saddle of lamb or beef; you had pudding; you had a savoury; and then you had fruit. Quite extraordinary— I can't think how we all ate so much."

The best part was that they didn't have to cook any of it. The food was prepared for them, in a place that they never visited, by people whom they never saw.

Early English kitchens were for cooking only (often separated from the main timber building for fear of fire). All storage, washing, peeling, and preparing was done in smaller satellite rooms; the scullery contained sinks and slop pails, the pantry was where food was stored, and the larder, a cool room with mesh-covered windows, contained meat storage. As kitchen staff increased, housekeepers, butlers, and footmen also had rooms off the kitchen where they worked and kept out of sight.

Sculptor Elisabeth Frink's brightly colored kitchen, ABOVE, *with the former stable walls used as room divider and hanging space. The central table is a butcher-block rolling cart. The Frink larder,* RIGHT. *Larders generally have very small windows to discourage flies and maintain a cool temperature.*

The kitchen of this Cornish farmhouse has original beams and slate slab floor. The dresser and cupboards are painted bright green because the owner "got fed up with pine."

The focal point of the kitchen was the hearth, later replaced by a massive, cast-iron range set into the wall like a fireplace. The German architectural historian Hermann Muthesius, writing in the early 1900s, noted that by this time continental cooks had realized that the most convenient cooking center should be freestanding, accessible on three sides.

"The English, however, with unshakeable obduracy, cling to their practice of wedging it between walls, so that every French chef who comes to England declares that he cannot possibly prepare even the simplest sauce on such a medieval contraption."

With due respect to Muthesius, the English may hardly have regarded this as a tragedy, their culinary skills being one of the few arts unresponsive to the influence of their neighbors across the Channel. But were he to return today, the kitchen would probably surprise him even more than the progress of English cooking. As many commentators have observed, probably the one thing most responsible for the enormous change in country-house life in England since World War I was the loss of the domestic class. Without those vast armies of cooks and kitchen staff, those entertainments could not happen. The kitchens were like evacuated barracks, useless, inoperable, obsolete. (The old kitchen at West Wycombe Park in Buckinghamshire was turned into a squash court in 1926, so its size can be imagined.)

Today's kitchen is probably more lived in than any other room in the English country house. Moved from its position as far away from the public entertaining rooms as possible (to keep those nasty cooking smells from permeating the refined atmosphere of proper society) into the heart of the house, it has become most frequently the room where family and friends eat. In many houses it has taken the place of the dining room,

which has itself been borrowed for a television room or playroom. What a change! Long gone are the huge, chilly, stone-floored caverns (often designed with barn-like ceilings to aid ventilation) filled with kettles, spits, hot plates, and iceboxes, where the servants produced meals for hundreds every weekend. Long gone are the processions of uniformed maids or footmen carrying food, carefully protected by gleaming silver covers, through the miles of corridors from kitchen to dining room, to be handed individually to each guest. Instead, it is the hostess herself who takes the roast beef out of the oven and on to the table before your very eyes.

Cooking has become the prerogative of the house-holder himself. Some houses can still draw in cooks from the outlying neighborhood, at least for the weekend house parties, but knowledge of cuisine has become as much a necessity for the cultivated person today as read-ing was in the 17th century. Kitchens are the new libraries, filled with cookbooks and herbals. Larders are generously stocked, easy for the cook to step in and out of. Any good houseguest should be able to contribute at least some element of cooking lore to the weekend mealtimes. This gentrification of cooking has led to imaginative ideas for setting tables—gardens, conserva-

Piano playing as well as cooking take place in this Dorset kitchen, LEFT, which belongs to author Lady Rachel Billington. Light and airy with huge flag-stones, it has ice-blue walls and rush chairs painted bright blue and white. On the left is the ubiquitous Aga stove.

This Wiltshire kitchen, BELOW, has an unusually wide pine table; a dresser stocked to overflowing with mugs, plates, jugs, and tureens; and, of course, a vase of fresh-picked flowers.

The kitchen of Abbotsworthy House, near Winchester, was once a schoolroom. An Aga replaces the old fireplace; at the far end, a French door opens into the garden.

A *larder is sometimes called an "English fridge." This is a rare type, the "hanging" larder, so designed in order to be out of reach of acquisitive rodents.*

T*he overall view of stencil artist Mary MacCarthy's classic country kitchen,* RIGHT, *in Norfolk. Her stenciling decorates the dresser cupboard doors. The round table covered in a cotton cloth, shelves displaying collections of crockery, old tins, trays, and spices give the room a lived-in feeling.*

S*tenciling also decorates her larder wall,* OVERLEAF, *while family treasures and plants look on from her kitchen window.*

tories, small corners of living rooms, are now designated as appropriate places to dine.

This revolution in social behavior has given the kitchen a set of new clothes. Before this century, it was considered unsuitable to display kitchen equipment, plates, cups, cutlery, on open shelves. The Welsh dresser, which first appeared in the 18th century in Shropshire and Staffordshire, became the perfect instrument of change. Usually made of pine, it had shelves and cupboard space just the right size for kitchenware, and with other additions suggested by the Arts and Crafts movement, represented the ideal piece of furniture in the new, natural, country kitchen.

Yet Muthesius would still feel somewhat at home. For although so much has changed in the way meals are now organized and prepared, almost all country-house kitchens still have one particular range "wedged between walls." Called an Aga (a manufacturer's name that has become as generic to the English as Hoover or Kleenex), it is a stove fueled by bituminous coal or anthracite (therefore requiring a chimney outlet), with burners and ovens that heat the room as well as the food. Muthesius might regretfully write it off as another example of the English "unshakeable obduracy." For the owners, it is a contraption of blissful practicality, since it provides perpetual and powerful heat (as long as it is lit) at a price people can afford, in places that may not, until recently, have received gas or electric supplies. (At Burghley, one of the grandest Elizabethan houses in England, there was no electricity in the attics until 1982.) The modern Aga has now been adapted for other forms of fuel such as gas and electricity, but it will be a long time before these replace the tried-and-true version so beloved by their owners.

THE TWO DIVINEST THINGS

THIS WORLD HAS GOT,

A LOVELY WOMAN

IN A RURAL SPOT!

❧ JAMES H. L. HUNT

1784–1859

SLEEPING

AFTER THE RATHER crude sleeping arrangements suffered by medieval knights and vassals, and the public-corridor style of sleeping endured by the Elizabethans, one would think that someone, the sophisticated King Charles II perhaps, might have come up with floor plans for more private sleeping quarters. But state bedrooms remained public places (not quite as public as French ones, which were used for huge social levees) well into the 17th century.

By the 18th century, country houses had been divided up into apartments, with separate bedroom, dressing room, and anteroom for the master and mistress of the house. It wasn't until this century that husband and wife were given the same bedroom, which they had to share. Before World War I such an idea would have seemed barbaric, quite apart from its obvious restraints on extramarital adventures. The image of prewar English country house weekends with everyone hopping in and out of everybody else's beds could only have arisen when married couples had separate

A *private bathroom at Deene Park in Northamptonshire with flowered porcelain, embroidered curtains, oak-paneled vanity, and Tudor engravings propped up against the ancient stone wall.*

This bedroom from Locko Park, Staffordshire, RIGHT, is given added luster by the four-poster bed frame and French inlaid wood dressing table.

The old chintz bed hangings and curtains dominate this guest bedroom, ABOVE, *at Aske Hall.*

Warm colors, a fragile chintz, and a substantial four-poster make for agreeable contrasts in Lady Zetland's bedroom, LEFT, *at Aske Hall, Yorkshire.*

bedrooms. Lady Sackville, Vita Sackville-West's mother, for instance, loved to entertain guests at Knole. According to biographer Victoria Glendinning, "She fitted up the spare rooms lavishly, each with its little brass frame on the door into which a card with the occupying guest's name was slotted. This was useful not only for administrative but also for amorous purposes: *Chacun à sa chacune,* as Mrs. Keppel is said to have remarked."

This attitude has a lot to do with upper-class English marriages, which frequently survive in spite of (or because of) the acceptance of dalliance. Since the parties concerned may be connected to a landed title, divorce is highly undesirable. Inheritance, after all, is what counts. A divorce threatens the continuation of a line, a principle to be pursued far more urgently than a little misplaced ardor. Kings of England have always known this. So have their wives. When King Edward VII was on his deathbed, his wife, Queen Alexandra, invited the king's longtime mistress, Mrs. Keppel, to the royal bedside—a

selfless act, indeed, but only to be expected under the circumstances. One of the more revealing remarks uttered during the abdication crisis over Wallis Simpson was, "Why doesn't the king just have an affair with her? Why must he marry the woman?"

Whether this approach is morally or psychologically satisfactory is beyond the scope of this book. It has little to do with the decoration of an English bedroom, which remains within the territory of the mistress of the house, whose taste it generally reflects. Most English bedrooms since the Middle Ages seem to have been furnished with a four-poster bed. Originally, protective curtains hung around the bed from railings suspended from the ceiling. The Elizabethans invented the four-post design, which was more effective in counteracting drafts and promoting privacy. (In Elizabethan houses, all rooms interconnected, making intimate affairs almost impossible to conduct.) The bed was the most precious piece of furniture in the Elizabethan house, and therefore the most ornately carved and richly hung, compared to the more austere furnishings in the rest of the rooms.

The four-poster continued to be fashionable until Victorian times, when it was suggested that the hangings promoted airlessness inside the bed, and therefore were not conducive to good hygiene. Beds without canopies were introduced instead. Many houses today still boast at least one four-poster, for their fine appearance remains undimmed by time; the hangings, however, are generally for decorative rather than practical purposes. Leading off from the mistress's domain (designated, needless to say, as the "master" bedroom), one may still find a dressing room, almost exclusively male, perhaps the last echo of the tradition of separate-sex sleeping quarters.

A guest bedroom in artist James Reeve's house in Somerset, ABOVE LEFT. *The fresh blue-and-white color scheme is pulled together by the ikat fabric bedspreads from Majorca.*

Lucy's bedroom, BELOW LEFT, *with horsy treasures, in Cornwall.*

An oasis of serenity, RIGHT, *in Sledmere House, created by the wallpaper-wrapped bath, soft fur rug, gentle colors, and flowers.*

MALE PRESERVES

A shooting lunch at Sledmere House (for men only). On the far wall, a portrait by 18th-century artist Sir George Romney of Sir Christopher and Lady Sykes, plus other family portraits and collections.
ABOVE: *Still the preferred method of surveying one's acres —on horseback.*

A MAN WAS lord of the manor. His son could inherit it. That, in a nutshell, is the story of women in England. Who can forget the desperate efforts of Vita Sackville-West, in our own century, to escape this tyranny and repossess the house she grew up in and loved above all things, Knole? "I want Knole," she wrote to her husband, Harold Nicolson, on her cousin's accession to the house at her father's death. "I've got an idea about it: shall we take it some day? . . . I've taken Dada's revolver. And the bullets." (The reason her cousin, Eddy Sackville-West, inherited, was that Vita's father had no male heir. Queen Elizabeth I had given Knole to Thomas Sackville in 1566; the family thereafter placed an entail on the property so that it could never be inherited by a woman.)

Guns in position, RIGHT, *at a shoot in Yorkshire. (In the film The Shooting Party, from the book by Isobel Colegate, the cognoscenti greatly criticized the filmmakers for placing the guns too close together.) Accomplished shots,* BELOW. *As Mary Clive has written, "Anyone could see that men had more fun than women."*

The captain's boot rack, RIGHT, *at Bereleigh, in Hampshire. Rubber boots, hunting boots, walking boots, and an elaborately carved, rare, stand-up boot remover. To the right, the captain's hat collection—for hunting, shooting, fishing, and promenading. The boxes are the familiar brown James Lock hat boxes—all labeled in the captain's own hand. Good guns,* BELOW, *carry good names— such as Henry Atkin Ltd.*

This is not to say that the wife had no role. As the Tudor writer Gervase Markham observed:

"[The lady of the manor] must be cleanly both in body and garments, shee must have a quick eye, a curious nose, a perfect taste and ready eare; (shee must not be butter-fingred, sweete-toothed, nor faint-hearted) for the first will let every thing fall, the second will consume what it should increase, and the last will loose time with too much nicenesse."

But as country house life developed, it became perfectly clear that many of its activities were designed to amuse, not so much the buds of London Society, as the flower of English manhood.

By the middle of the 18th century, the idea of Nature as a virtuous cause had taken root among the increasingly urbanized upper classes, and country activities such as riding, hunting, shooting, and farming were regarded as lofty pursuits. This notion, hand in hand

with the garden landscape movement, allowed men of breeding to spend much of their time roaming the English countryside, astride a horse, surrounded by dogs, admiring their land and communing with Nature in the most poetical and gratifying fashion. Many women were expert riders, and enjoyed fox hunting. But other sports were less accessible to the fair sex, if not totally beyond the pale.

By the 19th century, many house parties were organized for the specific purpose of shooting, or deer stalking, and estates became known for their good supply of game. (The Second Duke of Westminster put down something like 10,000 pheasants on his estate in Wales.) The ladies, unskilled with a gun, were either

Cricket, played by men (11 on a side), is considered by many to be the finest game ever invented for them.

excluded entirely from these weekends (their squeamishness about seeing birds systematically slaughtered rather spoiling the fun) or they learned to be one of the boys, as did the daughter of Baron Mildmay of Flete, in Devon. "With a really good shot," she reported, "you would quite often see four birds dead in the air at once, always shot in the head—none of that flutter-flutter-whump. Absolutely crump—dead. It was wonderful."

These exclusionist tactics naturally carried over into the social side of a sporty weekend. If ladies were present, they were allowed to join the large shooting lunches, but what could they contribute, not having downed a brace or two? Toward evening, when the guns returned home exhausted and exhilarated from their exploits, the female hangers-on could only stand and wait, and were probably roundly cursed for occupying badly needed bathrooms before dinner.

The dining room itself was until this century regarded as the man's domain. It was where he entertained rich and powerful visitors, either for self-advancement or reward for favor. (Hence the heavier, darker, more solid décor one still sees in many English dining rooms.) In the Middle Ages, it was considered that women would be distressed by the drunkenness at table. They should therefore be seated separately. Later on, it was still considered that women would be distressed by the drunkenness at table. Still later on, it was considered that women would be distressed both by the drunkenness at table and also by the smoke of the cigars. Women therefore retired to the upstairs boudoir or, more recently, to the drawing room, after the main meal had been served. This custom is mostly encountered now only at some formal occasions, when the ladies still withdraw after dinner to powder their noses and then take coffee in the drawing room.

An unusually fine billiard room from a house in Kent, with family pictures and two rocking horses. Billiard rooms have played their part in English history. Mary, Queen of Scots, loved to play, as did Napoleon. Byron began his affair with Lady Frances Webster, and Sir Winston Churchill proposed to Clementine, over billiards.

Meanwhile, at the all-male dinner table, risqué conversation can take place unhampered by propriety, while cigars are lit and a decanter of port is passed freely from hand to hand. (Freely, but the right way around the table, please. For the English, there is always a correct way of doing things.) Such a satisfying element of a man's life was this ceremony that many London clubs were designed to perpetuate it.

A *library fit for the setting of a Dickens novel*, LEFT — *books, files, scrolls, seemingly untouched for centuries—the classic working gentleman's den.*

T*his library,* ABOVE, *doubles as the study for a judge. His small walnut desk is almost buried in legal briefs. On the round 18th-century mahogany table are those two bibles of the English upper classes,* Burke's Landed Gentry *and* Kelly's Handbook to the Titled, Landed and Official Classes. *The painting of a white cockatoo is by the 19th-century artist H. Bright.*

And if the dining room displeased, why not move to the smoking room? Smoking is mentioned in the early 18th century, but did not take hold until Queen Victoria's consort, Prince Albert, and then her son, Edward VII, made cigars acceptable. The practice, however, was always regarded as unsuitable for the company of women, thus allowing Victorian men yet another excuse to escape polite society by retiring to have a smoke with the chaps. All-male smoking rooms became a common feature, therefore, of 19th-century country houses. Smoking also required its own uniform. The elegant, subtly colored velvet smoking jacket enhanced men's sense of themselves and, incidentally, limited the smell of tobacco to that particular garment. Billiard rooms also became a haven for men to play and smoke in, particularly during those *longueurs* during weekends plagued by bad weather or boring company.

The library, a family room in the 18th century, was restored to the menfolk in the 19th and 20th centuries. English country householders became far too busy with hunting, shooting, fishing, and the like to read much, but as they became more involved in farming and took upon themselves more and more the running of their land, libraries often doubled as studies, where estate and farm business was dealt with, away from the hurly-burly of the

house party activities. It is no accident that in detective stories, a genre that became immensely popular by the beginning of this century, it is to the library that Hercule Poirot and Lord Peter Wimsey invariably lure their suspects for an intimate little interrogation in private. (Murders always took place during a country house weekend, thus providing a plethora of suspects.)

Dressing rooms first appeared as late medieval appendages to bedrooms, each sex having his or her own, in which various activities, receptions, and the like took place. By the 19th century, women somehow had lost control of theirs, and were required to use more common territory, such as a morning room or drawing room, for their letter writing or tea parties. Dressing rooms became almost entirely masculine. In most country houses even today, if there is an extra room off the master bedroom, it is invariably assigned to the husband. Muthesius suggested a novel explanation for this development: that the bedroom was the woman's domain (it is certainly decorated as such), and the man simply her guest. In return, the man was granted his own room as compensation.

Even in these egalitarian days, it is impossible not to notice a bias in favor of the male in many English country houses. Who gets the dressing room? The downstairs cloakroom? The library? The hall shelves and boot rack? Even as most sexual distinctions begin to blur (everyone can smoke, drink, and do business, after all), decorating styles seem to exaggerate the separation. Chintz, flounces, puffy cushions, and lace—hers; wood-paneling, leather, Turkish carpets, and sporting prints—his. The English are largely responsible for so successfully maintaining these separate identities. Their houses show little sign of regret.

A *very personal male dressing room, showing the owner's sporting interests. The two cartoon pen-and-wash pictures on the bed are by Cecil Alding, a famous 19th-century sporting artist. On the silver tray is a collection of silver and ivory shoehorns and buckle fasteners; on the bed, a dyed-blue-green Hessian coverlet and kilim rug on top.*

69

Go anywhere in England, where
there are natural, wholesome, contented,
and really nice English people;
and what do you find?
That the stables are the real centre
of the household.
~ George Bernard Shaw

The F A

The wide sweep of the 18th-century stable buildings of Sledmere, RIGHT, *indicates their importance. Sledmere was until very recently one of the most famous studs in the country. Inside the stables,* LEFT, *a typical tack room, with old photographs and rosettes.*

PREVIOUS PAGE, *One of England's favorite family dogs, the labrador; and detail of* A Country House in a Wooded Setting, *watercolor by Michael Angelo Rooker (1746–1801).*

THE STERLING VALUES inherent in the idea of the family have never been extolled too highly in English culture. The literature, from Shakespeare to Jane Austen, has presented children as an annoyance at best, and traitors at worst. The English have always been ambivalent about parenthood. "He that hath wife and children hath given hostage to fortune," wrote the Elizabethan essayist Francis Bacon. "For they are impediments to great enterprises, either of virtue or mischief."

The only concession to family life can be traced to horseback riding. Ever since the Middle Ages, riding has always been a vital part of a proper English education, and well-bred children were taught the rudiments of horsemanship from the cradle. Fox hunting became the one sport "for the whole family." No English country house worthy of the name does not have a rockinghorse somewhere stored away. Horses (and to a lesser extent, dogs) were the one subject on which grownup and child shared the same passionate interest. The majority of the portraits that the Seventh Lord Cardigan had commissioned over the years to hang at Deene Park, for instance, were not of children, wives,

An 18th-century portrait of the hunter Sir Tatton Sykes, ABOVE, *with a groom and stable lad, from the Sledmere collection.*

mothers, or fathers, but of horses. There is a portrait of the immortal Ronald, the horse Cardigan rode in the charge of the Light Brigade, claiming pride of place alongside Prince, Sir Charles, Wanderer, Vanguard, Blackleg, Mars, Grandmaster, Chillianwallagh, and other favorites of Lord Cardigan's private cavalry. The priorities of the English paterfamilias can be inferred from the remark of Ben Marshall, a fashionable horse painter of the 19th century, who once explained, on his way to the races at Newmarket: "I have a good reason for going. I discover many a man who will pay me fifty guineas for painting his horse who thinks ten guineas too much for painting his wife."

Such was the interest in horses that the point-to-point was invented. This racing event is a cross-country steeplechase for amateurs, developed in the last century to allow the local gentry (who were buying horses to hunt on an increasingly grand scale) the opportunity to test their horses' potential by racing them from point to

Ronald, RIGHT, *the charger Lord Cardigan rode at the head of the Light Brigade during the infamous battle of Balaklava in 1854. Brought home in triumph (at least according to contemporary history), the horse lived to a dignified old age and died June 28, 1872. Ronald's tail, also preserved, hangs under the stairs in the main hall of Deene Park.*

point before making a purchase. The popularity of point-to-points led, in 1847, to the institution of the Grand National, the "Derby of the sticks," a race so rigorous that on at least one occasion only two horses finished.

Point-to-points are the antithesis of Ascot, being informal, lacking royal patronage, and open to anybody. Both sexes compete on equal terms, and must be amateurs. These race meetings, which take place in the spring, are closely connected to the local hunt, which runs them, and the condition of a horse's entry is that it must have been hunted during the season. But even at this relaxed sporting event, class will out. Attending a meeting, the observer cannot fail to notice an alarming

The various stages of a point-to-point, where amateur jockeys compete over monumental courses in all types of weather for modest stakes.

uniformity of costume that evidently marks one as a paid-up member of the point-to-point fraternity: the green "Wellies" (rubber boots), the Barbour jacket (a dark-colored, heavy cotton jacket with cord collar) or down jacket (often sleeveless), the earth-toned sweater, and the hat—an absolute must for both sexes—a racing trilby, tweed hat, or cap. The ultimate piece of equipment to perfect one's statement of pukka breeding is the shooting stick, on which one perches to watch the "princes of the pigskin" (amateur jockeys) urge their hunters past the finishing point.

Dogs rank equally high in the eyes of the English.

No country house worth its salt is without a dog. From earliest times dogs were used not only for hunting, but as rodent reducers, guards, and as now, as pets. While Lord Cardigan had his horses lovingly recorded for posterity, other artists did the same for dogs. "I would rather see the portrait of a dog that I know, than all the allegorical paintings they can shew me in the world," declared that paragon of culture, Dr. Samuel Johnson.

The painter William Hogarth was a famous dog lover and his portrait entitled "The Painter and His Pug" was the forerunner of many famous sitters and their four-legged friends. The Victorians took this passion to the limit. Queen Victoria's letters are studded

with references to the royal dogs, in particular Eos, Prince Albert's favorite greyhound, whose death was received with the shock due a major international incident. Sir Edwin Landseer, famous animal artist (he created the lions in Trafalgar Square) and Queen Victoria's favorite artist, became successful not, as Ruskin put it, "by the study of Raphael . . . but by a healthy love of Scotch Terriers." Queen Elizabeth II, with her devotion to her famous fleet of corgis, is merely carrying on an ancient royal tradition.

Prior to the 19th century, very little accommodation in the house was made for children. These small,

Racehorse portrait, OVERLEAF, *classical bust, blue-and-white porcelain umbrella stand, leather-studded sofa, wooden hunting-boot removers, black labradors— the insignia of an English country family.*

uninteresting creatures flitted from chamber to chamber and were ignored as much as possible until they were old enough to contribute to adult life. The Victorians took a more responsible line and invented the nursery, an area on the top floor of the house, as far away as possible from the grownups, where their children lived under the direction of spinster ladies called nannies. Boys in England went off to boarding school at an early age (seven or eight), leaving the girls with governesses upstairs.

The idea that parental influence is restricted to a few hours a week on horseback may not sit well in some psychiatric quarters, but the ways of the English nursery are not unsuited to the development of toughness and steadfastness of character. Many country houses still have nurseries and nannies (albeit younger and less starched than their predecessors) to instill these admirable qualities in their charges. Children of the ruling class still go to boarding school earlier than their American cousins. They also still remain devoted to the horses and dogs they grew up with. (If one were to examine the photographs young boarders have propped up on desks or bed tables, they would as likely show the family hunters as the family.) For the anthropologically inclined who may question this assertion, let us turn once more to interior decoration, where, as is so often the case, one may find the most accurate and revealing clues. Many children's rooms in a typical English country house are decorated, not with rock stars or sporting idols (although one might spot the occasional poster in a teenager's den), but with the rosettes won at local gymkhanas. These brightly colored satin ribbons convey the flavor of childhood for a certain class of English as vividly as the celebrated *madeleine* did for Proust.

English dogs for an English life. "Cats keep down mice,/And look quite nice,/But rarely engage the affections,/That go in canine directions." CLOCKWISE FROM UPPER LEFT: *Wild and domestic emblems of Heydon Hall, a wild boar and lurchers; the recently deceased bull terrier, Lamb Chop; an English terrier; "the country's going to the dogs"; profiles in courage—a lurcher and his stone ancestor, the greyhound; this Norfolk terrier prefers Wiltshire.*

This 17th-century portrait of a gentleman with his spaniel by an unknown artist vividly depicts the affectionate nature of the relationship.

This PORTRATVRE DOTH REPRESENT Elizabeth daughter of Sir
Thomas Brudenell knt: of Deine, first maried to Rice Griffin Esquire
defeated in Norwich fen, who was sonne and heire to Sr Thomas
Griffin of Brabrooke hall, and had ilue by him one daughter
named Mary. Second, she was maried to Sir Iames
Smith esquite of woden wawens in warwicke-
shire.

This is the loving memory of the aforesaid Mary
the onely daughter and heir to Rice Griffin & Elizat
she was maried to Thomas Marckham esquite
of Allerton in Sherwood, she had illue by him
sixtene children wherof ten weare sonnes and
six daughters.

*F*amily feeling at Deene Park. The large portrait, ABOVE, *is by an unknown artist of Sir Robert Salusbury, 1756–1817. Beneath him, our favorite horse, Ronald, makes another appearance. This time it's his hoof, mounted in silver, along with family photographs, a small portrait of Lord Robert Brudenell-Bruce, and an old-fashioned telephone.*

*T*he artist of this splendid Elizabethan portrait at Deene, LEFT, *not only records in writing that Elizabeth, eldest daughter of Sir Thomas Brudenell, produced 10 sons and 6 daughters, but also somehow manages to fit all 16 of them into his picture.*

A rocking horse, RIGHT, *with long straw tail, waits for a rider under the watchful eyes of a family ancestor.*

A collection of Staffordshire dogs, BELOW, *some with prey, surround Garibaldi.*

COME INTO THE GARDEN, MAUD,
I AM HERE AT THE GATE ALONE;
AND THE WOODBINE SPICES ARE WAFTED ABROAD,
AND THE MUSK OF THE ROSE IS BLOWN.
ALFRED, LORD TENNYSON

The G A

R D E N

The glorious gardens of Helmingham Hall, PREVIOUS PAGE, *near Ipswich, in Suffolk, and detail of* The Amateur, *watercolor by Frederick Walker (1840–1875). Helmingham Hall dates from 1480; the gardens have fine herbaceous borders and walks, a kitchen garden, and an ancient deer park of 400 acres.*

THE EARLIEST KNOWN gardens after the Dark Ages in England belonged to monasteries, with monks and nuns cultivating plots with vegetables, herbs, and flowers for decorating their churches. Henry VIII, the first giant of the Tudor dynasty, who wrested much of this land from the abolished monasteries, was himself a passionate gardener, and inspired his barons to cultivate their own gardens. Moreover, the Tudor aristocracy found the garden to be an excellent trysting spot for those practicing courtly love, a stylized form of "dating" during this period, which internalized passion and prohibited physical consummation—doubtless a necessity in the medieval manor, where the lord's male vassals vastly outnumbered the wives of the household.

Early Tudor gardens of the 15th century were mostly square in shape, with fine trees, shrubs, and flowers and arbors, with a pattern of interconnecting paths, some shaded by fruit trees, shrubs, or trellises. During the 16th century, knot gardens were introduced—geometrically laid-out patterns made in box, lavender, or rosemary, with brick paths, decorated with gravel or sand and small plants. Enter, once again, the French.

An outdoor staircase in Kent, LEFT, *planted with cotoneaster, moss, and alchemilla, with irises lining the walls and two cypress trees standing guard at the top. Another view,* FAR LEFT, *of the flowering steps. Climbing roses are trained over the sides, with urns and cupids adding architectural interest.*

Henry VIII is said to have sent his gardener to study François I's Fontainebleau when planning Hampton Court Palace. Thanks to the French influence, ever more elaborate designs were introduced, with arbors, statues, fountains, covered galleries, and separate little gardens, such as a rose garden or a pond garden. Elizabethan gardens were like outdoor rooms, containing avenues, walks, and vistas. The English also learned a great deal about plant materials from all their foreign travel, and introduced the fad for exotic planting.

At the beginning of the 17th century, it became fashionable to separate one's pleasure garden from the kitchen garden. (Until that time, vegetables and herbs grew alongside roses and hollyhocks.) William Lawson, a

The gardens at Hergest Croft, in Herefordshire. The designs include wide swaths of lawn punctuated by beds of dusky red wallflowers, called "Wenlock Beauty." Herbaceous borders contain irises, wallflowers, columbines, potentilla, and astilbe, with fruit trees for background. In the herb gardens are planted chives, mint, golden marjoram, chamomile, tarragon, hyssop, thyme, rue, chervil, winter savory, and sorrel, surrounded by box—just as the Elizabethans might have done it. Hergest Croft gardens have one of the finest collections of trees and shrubs in the country (including these old apple trees), as well as a wood with cascades of rhododendrons up to 30 feet tall.

Two-hundred-year-old apple trees in a Wiltshire kitchen garden, uncommonly espaliered in the shape of a circle.

very influential garden writer, published a book in 1618 in which he said, "It is meet that we have two gardens, a garden for flowers and a kitchen garden." Walls were built to separate the two, many of which remain today.

The French contributed another new element in the 17th century—the garden scheme. Lenôtre, the great designer of the gardens at Versailles, showed the English how to use vast acres of land as part of the layout of the garden, thus allowing romance to flourish at a much safer distance from the house. Estate owners took to the idea with enthusiasm and started cutting vast swaths out of the English countryside in order to make their grand parks, so much so that in at least one case the neighboring gentry were requested to continue the design on their own land (at their own expense), so as not to ruin the overall vista.

But the great gardening revolution in England came in the 18th century, when people threw off French formality and espoused the new cause of Nature, which meant opening up the parterres, or ornamental plots, and knot gardens to totally new arrangements of sculptured hills and valleys, with trees, steps, statues, obelisks, and even the occasional folly (an artificial, fanciful little castle, nook, or other construction).

People roamed through these landscapes, took picnics to secluded arbors, and generally behaved as though the French artist Watteau were making one of his brilliant pastoral paintings of the scene. Here is a description, written by one Dudley Ryden, of some gardens he visited in 1716:

"The situation of them is upon several hills that entertain the eyes with a variety of prospects. The parterre runs along between them with a pretty canal in the middle, at the end of which there are several fountains and a cascade from a

very steep hill of 224 steps, the finest in England except the Duke of Devonshire's."

Mr. Ryden enjoys an "agreeable" and "delightful" repast for several hours with friends in these surroundings. But alas, our hero's mood is quickly shattered:

"In this time Mrs. Marshall showed a great disregard of me and love of Mr. Powell; particularly she refused me a kiss when she gave him one immediately after. This put me in such a confusion and uneasiness that I could not bear it and was forced to take a walk by myself among the trees. Nor could I prevent the tears gushing out, that I was forced to be absent for almost an hour."

This kind of sentimental claptrap was precisely what Lancelot Brown, also known as Capability, most despised. Working as a gardener from about 1740 to his death in 1783, he regarded with scorn the Italianate silliness that had overtaken many gardens. Capability Brown abolished the formal garden altogether. He liked to "clump" groups of trees together in a bare landscape, preferring grass and wild flowers to plantings, a simple lake to fountains. Brown wanted simplicity, and that meant sticking to Nature's original designs, rather than adding artifice.

Many gardens and parks retain features of these 18th-century influences. The Victorians, especially those new to wealth, brought back the garden, with its variegated and picturesque flowers and shrubs. No discussion of English gardening is complete without mention of Gertrude Jekyll, that daunting woman who laid down rules of gardening that still apply today. She believed in making a plan of your garden, so that each plant, shrub, flower, and tree had a rationalized place in

Shells and rocks in a conservatory window form a decorative frame for potted geraniums and grandfather's bust, TOP.

Inside this potting shed at Sledmere a fire burns to keep the gardeners warm in winter, ABOVE.

An *indoor garden—
geraniums, fuchsia, and
campanula in colorful
profusion in a greenhouse
at Hergest Croft,* ABOVE.

A *planter on wheels,*
LEFT, *fills the window
with geraniums and
scented stock in happy
ignorance of the
foggy day outside.*

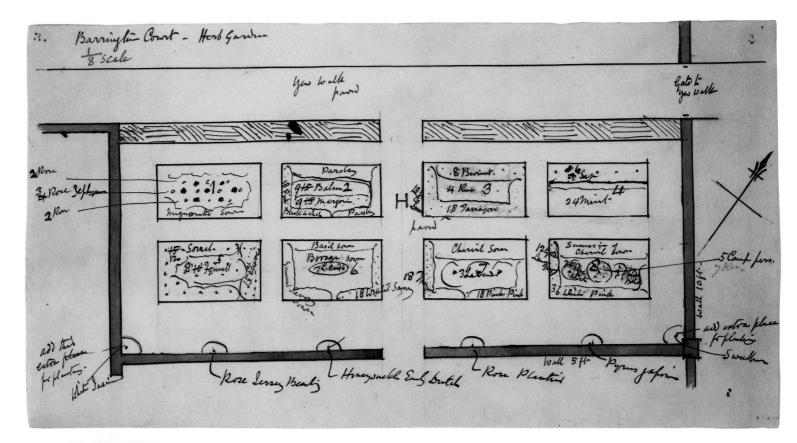

Barrington Court - Herb Garden
⅛ scale

the scheme of things. Her herbaceous borders set the standard forever after. Working with the famous architect Sir Edwin Lutyens, she produced gardens that, while maintaining traditions of the past, had a beauty, elegance, and simplicity that have never been surpassed. Katharine S. White, in her book *Onward and Upward in the Garden,* mentions a letter from the gardening writer Mrs. Mortimer J. Fox, which contains a telling vignette of her visit to Miss Jekyll's garden:

"While I was there, along came two maids with their streamers floating from their caps and their blue-and-white uniforms covered with large white aprons. They were carrying a large wash-basket which they held under one rosebush after another, and tapped the roses so the petals would fall into it."

Garden sketches drawn by Gertrude Jekyll, queen of the herbaceous border, the formidable Victorian who revolutionized English gardening with her ideas about mass planting, color "drifts," wild flowers, and plot planning.

Details of garden at Deene Park. Flowers against a brick or stone background—a typical form of English garden décor. Carved stonework, elegantly molded windows, and courtyards, such as this one, enhance the flowering plants and shrubs.

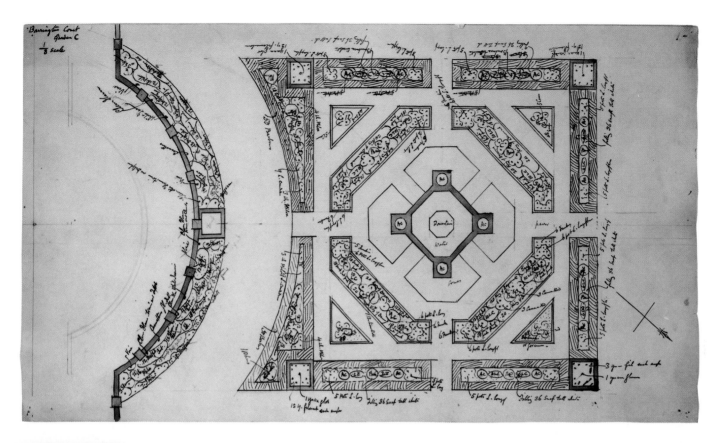

This intriguing assignment, as Mrs. White explains, was not merely to be tidy, for Gertrude Jekyll hated anything unnatural, but to provide material for her famous potpourris, which she produced right until the end of her life (she died at 89).

Gertrude Jekyll believed that a garden should be like a painting, and her herbaceous borders were meticulously planned for color and shape. But even she had to cope with the English climate. Over the centuries it was realized that, owing to the unfair vagaries of the English weather, the pleasures of the garden should be made available indoors. For some houses, this was provided by the conservatory, a glassed-in garden room with a plethora of scented plants and flowers, or a window garden, reminiscent of a greenhouse. Another alternative was simply—the vase of flowers. The English do not arrange flowers. In

Alchemilla, lavender, roses, peonies—some of the staples of an English herbaceous border.

England, the expression is to "do," not "arrange," implying that the flowers are stuffed in vases in some sort of impulsive pattern, falling as they may. There was a movement in the 1950s to create flower arrangements in the Japanese style, and Constance Spry became the doyenne of this new fashion, her teaching establishment for a time being the perfect finishing school for young debutantes. Little trace of her influence can be found in the country, where huge bunches of alchemilla, scented geraniums, annuals and perennials, grasses and weeds, are thrown together with reckless artistry according to the seasons.

Go into the most scruffy, unkempt, impoverished manor house in any part of England, and you will find an abundance of cut flowers in almost every room. While mice eat the books and mushrooms grow out of the paintings, flowers—on the piano, in the window, on the sideboard—hold up their heads in defiance of fate.

Artist James Reeve lives in a thatched cottage, ABOVE, *in Somerset (formerly a row of tanners' tenements) dating from the 16th century. His garden boasts a "folly"—a flower-covered gateway to nowhere,* BELOW. *Under an ivy-covered porch with climbing roses,* RIGHT, *are assembled a wicker umbrella stand and chair, plants in pots, and other objects required of the country gardener.*

A GEORGIAN HOUSE

LIKE SO MANY English country houses, this exterior is the result of many centuries of change. In Jacobean times, it was a farmhouse. In the 1780s, the owners decided to "gentrify" the place by adding two bays and a third story. Further additions were made later, including two wings built on by those mad house extenders, the Victorians. Many of their efforts were dismantled in 1949, and the house is now in roughly the same architectural form as it was in 1790.

This classically proportioned manor house, PREVIOUS PAGE, *looking out over a magnificent landscape of water and parkland (much of it laid out by the present owners), has two architectural faces. The newer side, with dormer windows and pretty doorway, is reflected in the water that stretches below. From inside,* LEFT, *pleasurable vistas unfold of fountains and water gardens, and at the end a folly in the form of a ruined temple.*

Entirely concealed from the main road, its glorious position can only be appreciated by those invited to the house. The building stands at the pinnacle of a magnificent vista of water and statues, and is surrounded by topiary, lawns, hedges, and beautifully constructed barns and stables. Built of rosy-colored brick, its rounded bays are covered with climbing roses.

The original doorway leads into a huge hall, with a large drawing room on the right and library/dining room on the left. In the drawing room the three ceiling-to-floor windows are crowned by papier-mâché pelmets added by the 18th-century owners who also created the bays. It has the typical lived-in quality of all these houses, filled with

In this hall, much history resides. The portrait over the mantel is of Henrietta, presumably the wife of one of the earliest owners. The unusually wide 19th-century chair to the left of the fireplace was specially designed for two men to sit in. In the 19th century anyone elected to Parliament had to be carried around his constituency by chair. On one occasion, two men (one of whom lived in this house) were elected—hence the twin-sized chair.

The dining room has invaded
the library, where family paintings, gold and red fleur-de-lis
wallpaper, and fine bookshelves
give it the feel of mellowness
and age. The inlaid-wood
chairs are Dutch. The curtains
are made of what is called
Utrecht velvet—a very heavy
fabric used frequently for its insu-
lating qualities and here trailing
on the floor to help prevent
drafts. (The fabric was never
actually made in Utrecht; the
term is really velours de trecht,
meaning a woolen velvet.)

There is an oriental flavor to this sitting room, evoked by the Chinese-influenced chintz, the leafy wallpaper, and the blue-and-white cachepot. The gilt valances are 18th-century additions made of papier-mâché.

books, magazines, and portraits inherited from the distinguished ancestors of the present owners.

The library, each wall of which is covered with books up to two-thirds of its height, has been turned into a dining room. In the library wall opposite the bay windows is a hatch into the kitchen, something doubtless undreamed of by its 18th-century owners.

The hall in the newer wing, reached by a long, drafty corridor, rewards the hardy visitor. It is as much a room

as any other in the house, with a fireplace, family portraits, and a central table for keys, messages, hats, and such. The view outside could hardly be improved upon.

The garden has many aspects. There are the formally landscaped water meadow and witty topiary, but there are also herbaceous borders with roses, honeysuckle, iris, potentilla, scented geraniums, veronica—flowers that are constantly picked and brought into this beautiful old house, infusing it with the feeling of the countryside.

This is known as the French bedroom, both for its colors and for the origins of the four-poster bed, which is decorated (with the slipper chair and wicker chaise) in a very old and rare chintz. The drop-leaf Regency table serves as a writing desk for guests.

This was once the front of the house, made more imposing by the added third story.

Above the doorway is inscribed "Henrietta Nobis" (her portrait hangs in the hall).

Pink roses, purple irises, and red geraniums decorate the warm brick of the bays.

The grounds of the house are as romantic as its exterior. The driveway, lined with hedges, leads from the house to the stables, which date from Georgian times.

The drive to the house and the stables are entered through magnificent carved wooden gates, providing a masterly preview of the house they so proudly protect.

The variety of gates in an English estate reflect the preoccupation with boundaries and enclosures.

A *more domestic part of the garden, with topiary. The classical busts decorated the Victorian part of the house, and were allocated surprising new homes when the wings were demolished. This smiling figure,* BELOW, *presides over an arbor filled with shrub roses, iris, and a small pond.*

CHANGELESS CHINTZ

NOTHING SO SYMBOLIZES the English country house interior as chintz. For anyone looking for a range of colors and designs, yet for more than that, for a feeling that comes from things English, chintz is the material that in an instant will summon up the best, prettiest, and most comfortable in English decorating.

Taking its name from the Hindu word *chint,* meaning variegated, chintz first appeared in the West as cotton cloth imported from India, "fast-printed with designs of flowers, etc.," as it is described in the *Oxford English Dictionary,* "in a number of colours, generally not fewer than five, and usually glazed." With the expansion of the Indo-European textile trade in the 17th century, chintz flooded the English market and was used not only for beds, windows, and chair cushions but also as dress fabric, often made up in waistcoats, robes, and women's gowns.

This invasion from the East did not sit well with the textile industry at home. In 1700, an Act of Parliament was passed in England banning the importation of all decorated stuffs from the Orient. (France also had problems, largely because of the domestic copying of these chintz designs; in the late 17th century an edict was passed forbidding the

The faded look of this chintz is not due to age. It is less than a decade old and comes from the Bennison fabric collection. Unlike most designers, who like to restore old fabrics to what they consider were the original colors, the late Geoffrey Bennison preferred to keep them exactly the same way he discovered them. This gives rooms furnished with his fabrics the feeling that they have been there hundreds of years. Bird and Basket is a pattern he took from an old chair cover.

Blue Roses, LEFT, *is an early Bennison design used at Sudeley Castle. Ribbons,* RIGHT, *was another tiny fragment found on a chair. Another popular pattern is Scatter Flower,* FAR RIGHT.

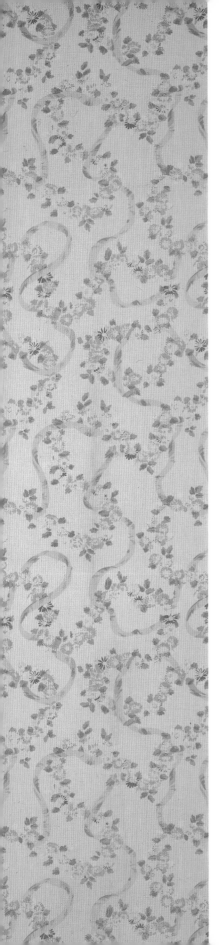

printing of cotton fabrics in France, and in 1686 all wood-blocks used in printing Eastern-style fabrics were ordered destroyed.)

As late as 1775, the famous actor David Garrick was complaining that customs officials had seized his wife's chintz bed hangings. But by this time, copperplate and roller-printing machines that could produce chintz patterns cheaply were in common use in Europe, thus putting an end to India's trade monopoly. (France at this time began to develop its own relation to chintz, Toile de Jouy, which became equally popular.) Once chintz began to be mass-produced, however, printing quality rapidly deteriorated. With the discovery of aniline dyes in 1856, chintz designs became even cruder and coarser, hastening their decline in the eyes of connoisseurs. One wonders if the word *chintzy* meaning "cheap" originated at this time. (It was these same aniline dyes, oddly enough, that inspired the brilliant weaving revolution among the Navajo Indians, who for a decade or so produced "Eye Dazzler" blankets that are rare collector's items today.)

While the domestic textile industries began to flourish, chintz was being exported in large quantities to America, the colonists having a natural preference for English fashions. In 1800 there are records of London drapers recommending to Americans "packages" of coordinated chintzes that could be used for a variety of decorating purposes. Pattern cards and swatches were sent over by ship for customers to choose from; in 1774, for instance, the price of a five-color calico with a purple ground was 40 shillings for a 12-yard piece. One of the finest chintz collections in America is at Winterthur in Wilmington, Delaware. Henry Francis du Pont was a keen enthusiast of English chintzes and inherited a set of printed bed hangings called "Ducks" made in 1765–1775 at Bromley Hall, England, that can be seen in the Franklin Room at Winterthur.

Chintz continued to suffer a decline in quality at home

until the late 19th century, when William Morris and the Arts and Crafts movement restored its original quality by means of special reproduction. Morris returned to the original "document" prints (preserved in museums and in private collections) and meticulously re-created their designs and colors, printing them not only on cotton but also on silks and linens. Liberty & Co. took up his designs at the same time as the Art Nouveau fashion began to spread. The birds, flowers, and sinuous shapes of chintz brilliantly satisfied the contemporary passion for natural forms.

Perhaps the person most responsible for the continued popularity of chintz in this century is an English decorator called John Fowler, originally the partner in the decorating firm of Colefax and Fowler with Lady Sybil Colefax, and after 1945 with Nancy Lancaster. In addition to being a historian of decoration, and therefore knowledgeable about patterns from the past, Fowler (who died in 1977) was a designer of considerable talent, and his own chintzes, such as Bowood (first appearing in 1938), have added to the vast library of chintzes available. He rarely designed from scratch: his inspiration would come from a design on an 18th-century bowl, a fragment of wallpaper, or an antique gown. Another important contributor to the chintz canon is the late Geoffrey Bennison, whose deliberately aged designs, on finest-quality cotton and linen, have graced many a famous room both in Europe and America.

John Fowler's partner, Nancy Lancaster, working after the war in England, encouraged the use of chintz in both grand and modest houses, believing that these cheerful and elegant cottons could adapt to any surroundings. She understood that chintz could be used to relax a room and relieve it of too much freight from the past. To achieve the natural, faded look that English chintz so often has, she is known to have soaked her fabrics in tea.

Today, authentic English chintz may be identified by the deep and subtle colors and exuberant flower and bird

Sir Arthur Liberty founded the store that bears his name in 1875, specializing in orientalia and products of the Arts and Crafts movement. He was an innovator in the design of dress and furnishing fabrics, of which these are representative. Liberty designs remain in great demand today. These typical examples from the Liberty pattern book are Clandon, LEFT, *and Melrose,* ABOVE *and* BELOW.

designs, often with an oriental flavor. (No one has counted the patterns, but there must be well over 1,000 in circulation.) English chintzes favor soft, earthy shades, unlike the sharper, brighter palette preferred by the American market. Many carry a pale brown or "tea" background. Funnily enough, although chintz is thought to be the *sine qua non* of every English interior, there is less of it to be seen in the rooms represented in this book than might be expected. There may be a cushion here, a slipcover or curtain there, but not much more. It is perhaps true to say that while in the mind an English room is filled with chintz, the reality, as with so many things English, is modified by restraint.

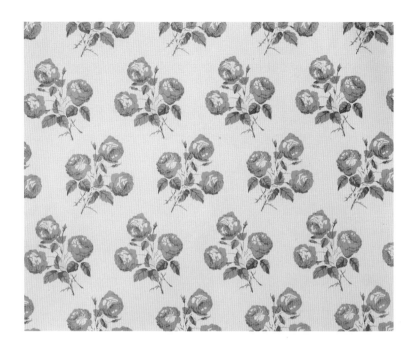

Thanks largely to the keen eye of John Fowler, Colefax & Fowler chintzes are some of the most beautiful and classic in the world.

CLOCKWISE FROM FAR LEFT, *Paeony; Bowood, a John Fowler chintz dating from the 1930s; Hydrangea, from the new Jubilee Collection; Tree Poppy; and Eugenie.*

HEYDON HALL

UNIQUE EVEN IN England, this house sits at the end of a cul-de-sac, in an untouched corner of Norfolk where no through traffic has ever disturbed the almost feudal atmosphere of the village. Readers of Barbara Pym will at once feel at home here. House, park, church, cottages— all belong to the owners of Heydon, a house built in 1580 by Henry Dynne and lived in by the Bulwer family since the 18th century. The village is as old and unspoiled as the house, some cottages in what is known as Widow's Walk having received indoor plumbing only in the last 25 years. The little 14th-century church nestles at the side of the village green, which was once the forum for a medieval market.

It is difficult to imagine a more perfect example of Elizabethan architecture than Heydon Hall, PAGES 120–121, *with its wonderful chimneys, gables, and brickwork. Nearby, Newhall Wood, looks innocent as a sea of bluebells in early spring, but was a place of death for local poachers just a century and a half ago.*

The *south porch of Heydon church,* RIGHT, *built in 1390, with the priest's room above. The tower behind was built in 1470, out of the same stone, which came from Barnack quarries.*

The *cottages being painted here,* LEFT, *were given pediments in the 18th century as part of a remodeling plan to give the village uniformity and form, by William Wiggett Bulwer, the first of the family to own Heydon. Heydon is a frequent winner of "perfect village" awards,* CENTER. *The kind of issue most likely to exercise its 300 inhabitants is whether to cut the grass on the green or leave it wild to encourage increasingly rare buttercups to grow.*

The *village green,* RIGHT, *once a medieval market, now boasts a Victorian well and neat rows of cottages.*

The drawing room, LEFT, *glows with its red walls (the paint matching an original wallpaper), upholstery, and rugs. A large window in an equally large bay is typical, reflecting the Elizabethan hunger for light. Not shown is a huge carved fireplace that balances the high ceilings and window.*

The porter's chair in the hall at Heydon—*an early-1800s studded leather shrine for the ancestor of today's doorman. Behind it, a beautiful canvas screen, painted on both sides with pictures of dogs and cockerels, dating from the late 1770s. Such screens, designed to keep out drafts, were commonplace from earliest Georgian times.*

The kitchen, ABOVE, was a study in the 19th century, hence the inset mahogany book-cases (now holding china), the Victorian trophies that still hang over the stove, and the William Morris wall-paper. The room is 30 by 24 feet—a fine size for an eat-in kitchen that is also often used for informal dinner parties.

A massive pine dresser, LEFT, holds most of the family's daily needs in terms of cups, plates, and mugs, plus a collection of Mason's Ironstone.

A room for boots, flowers, hunting equipment, and other outdoor paraphernalia, RIGHT. This would be called a "mud room" in an American house.

Heydon Hall is an Elizabethan jewel box of a house, with magnificent chimneys, windows, and bays, and yet containing only nine bedrooms—very small compared to many others of the period. Needless to say, by 1923 it had accumulated an orangery, west tower, east wing, and ballroom—grandiose Victorian additions only recently, and with a certain amount of soul-searching, demolished.

Inside, the house expresses the comfort that comes from much history and no self-consciousness. The Red Drawing Room's warm colors were suggested by an old

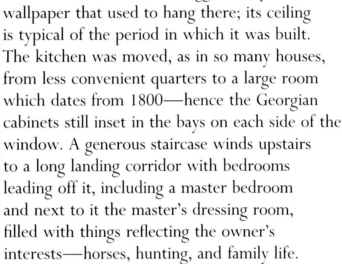

wallpaper that used to hang there; its ceiling is typical of the period in which it was built. The kitchen was moved, as in so many houses, from less convenient quarters to a large room which dates from 1800—hence the Georgian cabinets still inset in the bays on each side of the window. A generous staircase winds upstairs to a long landing corridor with bedrooms leading off it, including a master bedroom and next to it the master's dressing room, filled with things reflecting the owner's interests—horses, hunting, and family life.

The garden, mostly generous lawns and herbaceous borders, has some charming statuary, but the strength of the house comes from its position in its Norfolk landscape, rooted to its park and pastures for over 400 years. Newhall Wood, a few minutes' walk from the house, was the scene of one of the most notorious local events of the last century, when in 1826, 13 poachers were caught here and sentenced to death. The extremity of this sentence only shows to what lengths the famous English judicial system allowed landowners to go to protect their property. Nor were the country's game laws changed, shameless as they were, until well into the 20th century.

Captain and Mrs. William Bulwer-Long, LEFT, *are keen riders, the captain having been a well-known amateur jockey. These horses are being directed along a driveway that leads from the stables, then past the house to the village. In other words, there is no through road past Heydon; it remains a pocket of untouched history.*

A boy plays a tune on his pipe, RIGHT, *to this side door of Heydon Hall, decorated by an Elizabethan coat of arms.*

The master bedroom, ABOVE, is decorated with pale yellow walls
and honeysuckle chintz. The bed hangings are lined with
tiny pink-and-white checked glazed cotton, and the posts of the
four-poster covered in padded chintz (all made in the village).
The fireplace, BELOW, is dominated by the portrait of a family
ancestor, Elizabeth Dering, dated 1751. At each end of the mantelpiece, oval framed lithographs are propped up on porcelain mugs.

A Georgian mahogany bookcase inset into the wall of this spare
room, RIGHT, reminds guests that the room was once part of a
huge upstairs library. Engravings by famous artists (here, Claude
Lorraine's view of Rome's Pamphili Palace) were popular country
house wall decorations in the 18th and 19th centuries.

HEYDON HALL
DOLLS' HOUSE

HEYDON HALL IS the proud possessor of one of the oldest dolls' houses in the country, even older than the famous one attributed to Thomas Chippendale in Nostell Priory, in Yorkshire, dated 1740–1745. The Heydon dolls' house was given by Queen Anne to her goddaughter, Ann Sharp, in 1696, when she was five years old. Ann Sharp's father was Archbishop of York, and the queen was a friend of both Ann's parents. Ann was one of 14 children; she died in 1771, and the dolls' house has been handed down through descendants with almost no changes.

The town house has nine rooms on three floors. It is clearly a house of quality, with the fictional residents, Sir William and Lady Rockett, people of consequence. They have a butler ("Roger, ye butler"), "Hannah, ye housekeeper," a nurse, and a footman, although not the kind of footman we know today, but the man who ran on foot before the sedan chair or carriage. All the fittings, in their striking detail, are original, and the wallpaper is older than any to be found in England. This treasure is kept in the hall at Heydon, where visitors may examine it by appointment. Please write to Mrs. William Bulwer-Long at Heydon Hall, Heydon, Norfolk.

With doors open, the astonishingly detailed decorations of this dolls' house, dating from 1696, dazzle the eye. The central room of the third story is the dressing room of "William Rockett," lord of the manor, in which hangs a large framed wax bust of Mother Shipton, the Yorkshire witch, said to have been born in 1486. Hanging from the ceiling of this room is an elaborately carved cedar chandelier, with sconces for 18 candles, enclosed in a glass globe.

Ann Sharp's miniature town house is divided into three floors and an "attic" of treasures. The bottom floor belongs to the servants (housekeeper on the left, butler's pantry in the center, servants' hall on the right). The middle floor is the entertaining suite—drawing room, hall, and kitchen. Upstairs, the bedroom, dressing room, and nursery.

A *party is going on in the drawing room,* FAR LEFT, *consisting of "Lady Jemima Johnson," "Mrs. Lemon," and "Lord and Lady Rockett."*

T*he Rockett kitchen,* LEFT, *with utensils, pewter plates, and on the spit, a suckling pig. Roast suckling pig was very popular with the gentry during the reign of Queen Anne.*

D*etails of the pewter and china, all to perfect scale,* FAR LEFT *and* LEFT, *including a cheese grater that could have been made yesterday. The candlesticks on this table are Charles II silver, with the date mark 1703, and are 2⅛ inches high. Many of these brilliantly made miniatures were produced as travelers' samples and later relegated to the children.*

T*he master bedroom, belonging to "Lady Rockett,"* BELOW FAR LEFT *(all the inhabitants' names are pinned to their person). Note the glamorous pink-striped brocade bed hangings, and blue-and-white porcelain.*

A*nother fine bed,* LEFT, *this time hung with green silk and silver lace embroidered hangings, decorates the nursery. (Nanny obviously belonged to a higher social echelon than the housekeeper, whose greatly inferior room can be seen belowstairs.) The baby's cradle is trimmed in ivory filigree.*

A *detail of the drawing room,* LEFT, *showing the magnificent gold-leaf wallpaper, original to the house. The portrait is of Queen Anne.*

P*art of the "attic" collection,* BELOW, *more mementos of the days of Queen Anne. The chased leather muff box on the left contained a sable muff that was presented to Ann Sharp's mother by Queen Anne. The box is very small, 8 inches high and 5½ inches in diameter, showing how tiny people's hands were in the 17th century. (Gloves of the period confirm this observation.) Behind the muff box is an elegant pair of satin slippers.*

THE OLD RECTORY

BUILT IN THE 17th century, this charming house is typical of the sort lived in by men of the cloth. In those days, parsons and rectors were still regarded as gentlemen of the most refined sort, a hangover from the period when the clergy, thanks to their advanced literacy, were second only to kings in power and authority. Many of the prettiest houses in England are those attached to the village church, and although some have been relinquished and turned over to private ownership (as in this case), those that remain offer perhaps a small enticement or consolation to those underpaid and much-maligned representatives of the Church of England today.

The Old Rectory in Holt is a simple house, with small, well-proportioned spaces more suited to ecclesiastical than secular entertainment. The most interesting

The south-facing garden, RIGHT, *overgrown with honesty, spurge, and bright red poppies, provides a romantic setting for afternoon tea.*

The side door into the garden, ABOVE LEFT, *hinting at the wild flowers and woodland surrounding the house. The graceful front door,* ABOVE RIGHT, *reflects the harmonious architecture of the period.*

From the wild to the domestic —a Norfolk bluebell wood, PREVIOUS PAGE, *provides an unrestrained contrast to this charmingly self-contained facade. The house dates from the 17th century, but its Georgian front was added by an upwardly mobile parson in 1725.*

room, architecturally speaking, and the favorite of its owner, Lady Harrod, is the oval-shaped Red Room, originally the rectory dining room. As always, an alarming distance from the kitchen, it is now used as a library and winter sitting room. The room is dominated by an old Steinway piano, said to have belonged to Henry James.

The beautiful setting of the house is the result of much planning by previous parsons, who planted trees, a woodland belt for a Sermon Walk, a walled kitchen garden, and a pond. Lady Harrod describes its different aspects:

"Although the main road is very close, it cannot be seen from any window. The house sits right in the middle of its five and a half acres of garden and woodland, and in the spring the east and south windows look onto a sea of snowdrops. From the dining room and the kitchen windows on the north side the view is, suitably, of asparagus beds and globe artichokes, and an old apple tree with a huge Albertine rose."

The stone-floored hall and finely curved staircase, LEFT, hung with portraits and memorabilia. Lady Harrod's pride and joy, her log basket, RIGHT, with a view beyond to the dining room and kitchen.

Red-striped wallpaper and red upholstery, ABOVE, add warmth to the semioval library. The Steinway, made in New York in 1878, in addition to its possible link to Henry James (who knew Lady Harrod's mother-in-law), provides a useful surface for old family photographs. The fireplace, RIGHT, is marble, decorated with blue-and-white tiles.

A *guest room,* LEFT, *with the obligatory writing table. "Writing-tables are what I see when I think of my own home," wrote Lady Mary Clive. "Good visitors were supposed to write letters all the morning. . . . These writing-tables were kept in mint condition and they all had the light coming from the left and were supplied with everything that the most captious visitor could require."*

L*ady Harrod's bedroom is filled with light, enhancing the delicate mauve wallpaper and violet-patterned fabric. Family photographs, portraits, and books give this room an intensely personal quality.*

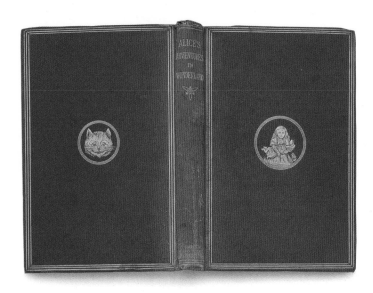

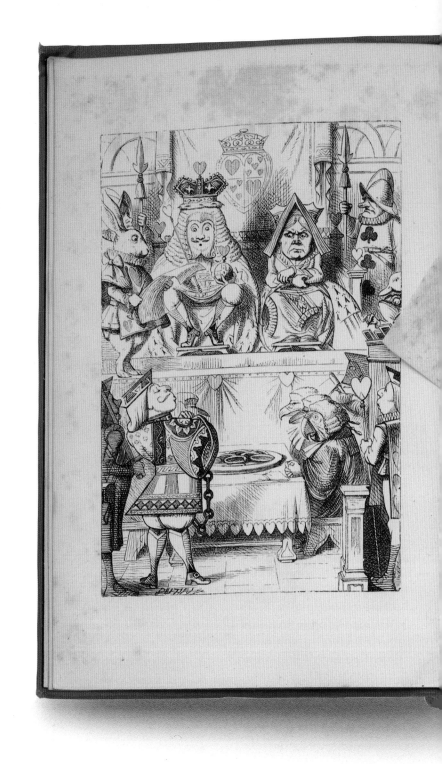

Engraved on every child's heart as well
as in the definitive Alice—
the pictures of Sir John Tenniel.
The original binding, ABOVE,
and title page, RIGHT.

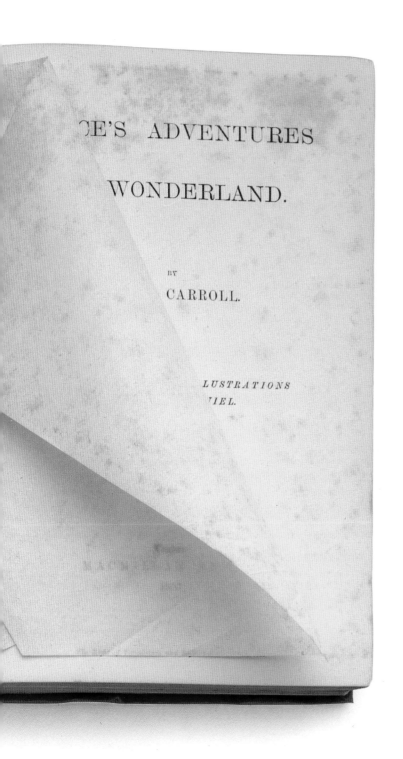

A CHILD'S COUNTRY OF BOOKS

WHILE ENGLISH CHILDREN may not have enjoyed the primacy of place in the family given to their European or American cousins, their reading matter was always taken with the utmost seriousness. Nursery rhymes date back many centuries, their sometimes mysterious-sounding symbolism probably originating in very real history. "Ring-a-Ring-a-Roses," for instance, has been compellingly interpreted as a rhyme describing the symptoms of the plague; "Mary, Mary, Quite Contrary" may well have been about Mary, Queen of Scots. Fairy tales, as well as expressing deep-seated fears and fantasies, were used as morality lessons, designed to inspire obedience and submission. Illustrations of these stories were often beautifully and memorably rendered by distinguished artists.

Life was frequently bleak and lonely for the children in 19th-century fiction. Parents are often struck down by cholera (evidently a major fear in the Victorian mind; many educated families had taken up posts in the far-flung reaches of the British Empire where exotic diseases ran rampant). The dispossessed orphans are forced to live in large, scary houses with distant relatives and an unsympathetic nurse—the more common 19th-century address for nanny (Mary Poppins came as quite a revelation to a whole generation of children). Life is a series of hideous trials and dangers, people weep copiously into cambric hankies, and happy endings come only to those who are "good."

The poet who brought all these elements together in a hilarious series of volumes called *Cautionary Tales* was Hilaire Belloc (1870–1953). Belloc, an Anglicized Frenchman, threw himself into English life, politics, and literature and gave children a world of wonderfully naughty boys and girls who learned about Good Manners the hard way. Who could forget Matilda, who told such Dreadful Lies, or Henry King, whose chief defect was chewing little bits of String, or rude and wild Rebecca, who, like all of them, came to a bad end?

> Her funeral Sermon (which was long
> And followed by a Sacred Song)
> Mentioned her Virtues, it is true,
> But dwelt upon her Vices too,
> And showed the Dreadful End of One
> Who goes and slams the door for Fun.

Reading some of this children's literature today, two things strike the modern reader. One is the unshakable presence of class. Most of these books were written for and by the upper middle classes and the stories are peopled by characters with names like Marmaduke and Pamela, who have a nurse, a cook, various chambermaids, and the other appurtenances of a comfortably off family household. The children's attitudes to these servants, and indeed to anyone who smacks of working-class roots, is of unassailable superiority, mingled with condescension. In *The Cuckoo Clock,* by Mrs. Molesworth, for instance, our

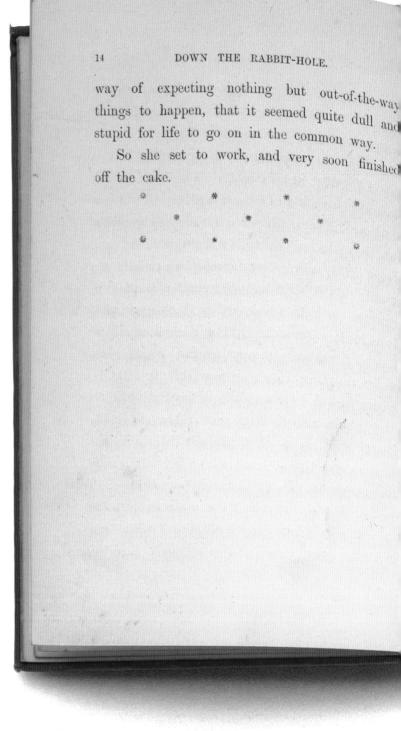

A *typical chapter title,* ABOVE RIGHT, *from* **Alice in Wonderland, *with Tenniel illustrations*.**

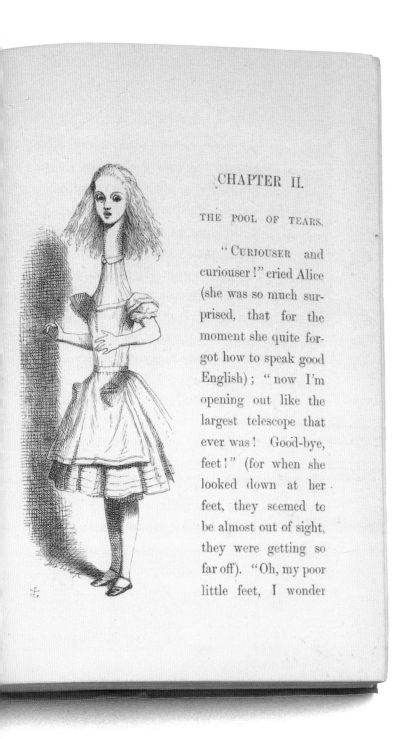

CHAPTER II.

THE POOL OF TEARS.

"CURIOUSER and curiouser!" cried Alice (she was so much surprised, that for the moment she quite forgot how to speak good English); "now I'm opening out like the largest telescope that ever was! Good-bye, feet!" (for when she looked down at her feet, they seemed to be almost out of sight, they were getting so far off). "Oh, my poor little feet, I wonder

George MacDonald's legendary tale, RIGHT, *about the ageless spinning princess as depicted by James Allen.*

heroine, Griselda, meets a young boy in the woods, who allows as how he has a nurse. "Have you a Nurse?" Griselda asks in relief. "She had not felt at all sure what SORT of little boy he was, or rather what sort of people he belonged to." After this reassurance, she feels free to play with him.

The other element of many of these books is their infallible sense of place. Houses, rooms, and gardens are described with meticulous attention to detail. Here is a description of the country house where the Bastable family stayed, from E. Nesbit's *The Wouldbegoods.*

"The Moat House was the one we went to stay at. There has been a house there since Saxon times. It is a manor, and a manor goes on having a house on it whatever happens. The Moat House was burnt down once or twice in ancient centuries—I don't remember which—but they always built a new one, and Cromwell's soldiers smashed it about, but it was patched up again. It is a very odd house: the front door opens straight into the dining-room, and there are red curtains and a black-and-white marble floor like a chess-board, and there is a secret staircase, only it is not secret now—only rather rickety. . . ."

The first page of *Us, an Old Fashioned Story,* another masterpiece by Mrs. Molesworth, who wrote over one hundred books for adults and children, carries a description of the drawing room that has the clarity of a photograph:

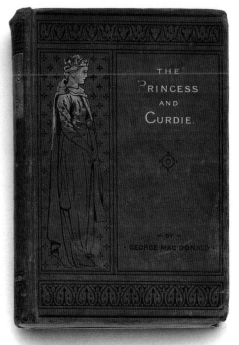

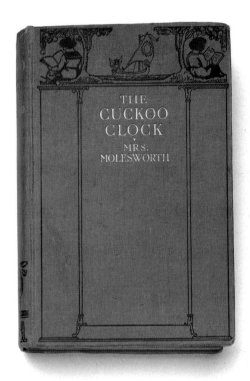

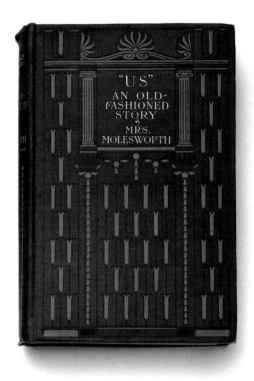

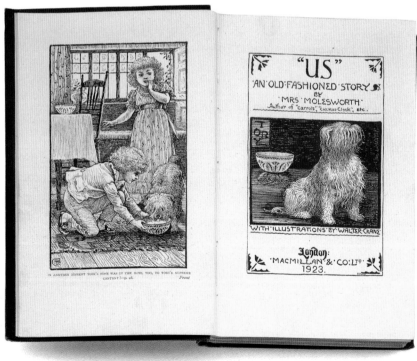

148

"There was a round table in the middle; there were high-backed mahogany chairs against the wall, polished by age and careful rubbing to that stage of dark shininess which makes even mahogany pleasant to the eye, and with seats of flowering silk damask whose texture must have been VERY good to be so faded without being worn; there were spindle-legged side-tables holding inlaid "papier-mache" desks and rosewood work-boxes, and two or three carved cedar or sandal-wood cases of various shapes. And most tempting of all to my mind, there were glass-doored cupboards in the wall, with great treasures of handle-less teacups and very fat teapots, not to speak of bowls and jugs of every form and size. . . ."

Mrs. Molesworth's prose is studded with sociologically revealing detail; Grandmama, for instance, whose drawing room is described above, possesses a tea set made of Chinese Export porcelain that is so precious that she will not let the maid touch it, but carefully washes the delicate cups and saucers herself after tea. This early literary exposure must have bred in children a kind of feeling for their land and family heirlooms that is generally regarded as part of the national character.

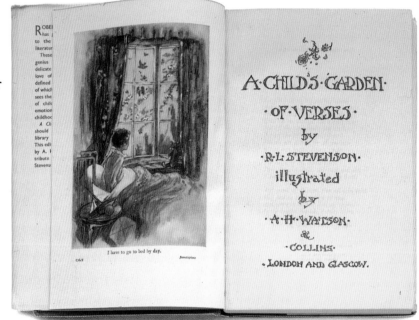

The other salient element in many of these stories is the constant influence, and in many cases redemptive power, of the natural world and of the countryside. *The Wind in the Willows, The Water-Babies, The Secret Garden,* the work of A. A. Milne, Beatrix Potter, Arthur Ransome, Beverley Nichols, Edward Lear—their themes reflect the last century's interest in the Arts and Crafts movement, with its emphasis on the virtues of Nature, of country life, and as a corollary, of the innocence of children. It comes as no surprise that Walter Crane, one of William Morris's most talented disciples, and a painter and textile designer of European renown, should have spent so much of his working life designing wallpapers for nurseries and illustrating children's books. (Crane evidently enjoyed this work: "I was in the habit of putting in all sorts of subsidiary detail that interested me," he wrote in his memoirs, "and often made them the vehicle for my ideas in furniture and decoration.")

Belloc devoted a splendid series of rhymes to animals, including the dromedary, the frog, the whale, the vulture, and the tiger:

> Mothers of large families, who
> claim to common sense,
> Will find a Tiger will repay the
> trouble and expense.

Another expression of this belief in Nature can be found in the passion of English children's writers for making up stories that required maps, as exhibited in the brilliant rabbit world of Richard Adams's *Watership Down*, and culminating in the astonishingly elaborate topography of J. R. R. Tolkien's *Lord of the Rings*.

It is the illustrations, of course, that make the deepest impression on a child's mind and linger longest in the memory of the adult. John Tenniel, Arthur Rackham, E. H. Shepard, Beatrix Potter, Kate Greenaway, Randolph Caldecott, and more recently Lillian Hoban, Nicola Bayley, Michelle Cartlidge, Helen Craig, and Charlotte Firmin have provided images of such lasting poignancy that houses, animals, gardens, and fields become permanent inhabitants of the English imagination.

Maps drawn by J. R. R. Tolkien for **The Hobbit** *for the front and back endpapers,* RIGHT.

Opening pages of a map from **A Squirrel Called Rufus,** BELOW LEFT, *by Richard Church. Pooh's map of the world, drawn with the help of Pooh's illustrator, E. H. Shepard, for the endpapers,* BELOW RIGHT.

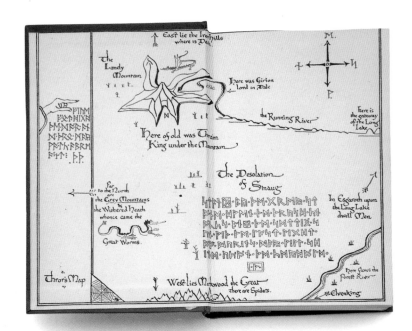

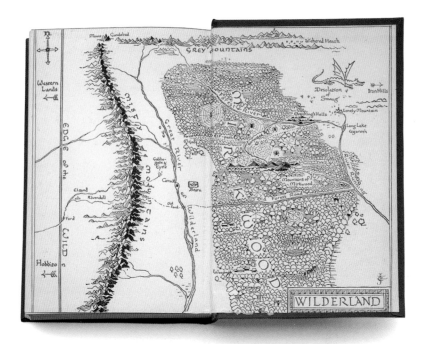

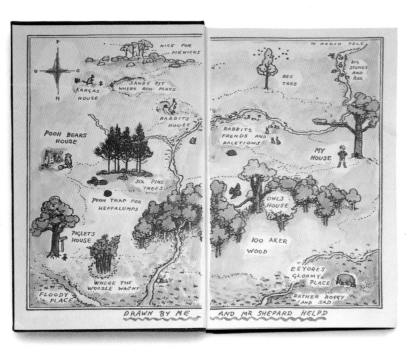

BLACKLANDS

UNLIKE MANY OTHERS in this book, this elegant
Georgian house has not belonged for many generations to
the same family. An 18th-century country gentleman's
house, beautifully situated beneath the Marlborough
Downs in Wiltshire, it suffered the same fate as so many
other Georgian masterpieces when delivered into Victorian hands. The northern-facing rooms, their softer light
kinder to Victorian watercolors and upholstery, were
enlarged and given Venetian windows. The Georgian win-
dowpanes were changed to modern plate-glass ones, and
the modest driveway was rejected in favor of a new, long,
pretentious one with a fancy lodge built at the end of it.

When the present owners bought it in 1973, only
the ground and first floors were lived in. The rest was in

The north entrance, LEFT, decorated with daisies and honeysuckle, with a view through the hall to the garden and river Marden. A stone guardian, RIGHT, at the entrance crouches beneath a panoply of daisies.

charred ruins from a fire occurring during World War II. The courageous buyers, aided by architect Stuart Taylor and a good local builder, set to work to take out Victoria and put back George. The backstairs, cobwebbed passages, butler's pantry, 19th-century kitchen, servants' quarters, were all removed. Georgian moldings, cornices, chimneypieces, and windows were restored. Judicious use of paint, fabrics—some suggested by decorator David Vicary, onetime colleague of John Fowler—and the owners' collection of pictures and books, turned a series of dingy and depressing spaces into graceful and welcoming rooms.

Perhaps color is the most striking feature of the interior of the house. The paint on all the walls has been stippled on by painter Derek Norris in artist's oil paints, with a scumble glaze —a dark wash over a lighter one. This technique both intensifies the color yet also gives it a translucent effect. Chintz is used sparingly but to telling effect. The furniture includes Conran's wicker mixing with Victorian mahogany, gilt with pine.

The other essential quality that informs these rooms is their personal feeling—and that comes to a large extent from the pictures that hang on the walls. The owners grew up in an environment dominated by the Pre-Raphaelites, William Morris, and Lord Berners, and this taste is reflected in the paintings and objects filling their house. None of the paintings is by a "famous" artist. The owners' interests lie in English vernacular architecture and art, so many of the pictures are English and depict English scenes. They buy dusty canvases in the Portobello Road, attracted by the subject matter or a color palette. They like jokes, and buy for fun. "Art never lets you down" is their maxim and it shows in every corner of the house.

Blacklands, PREVIOUS PAGE, with its Victorian pediment shelters behind the protective shadow of the Wiltshire Downs. The other side of the house overlooks gardens and a modest waterfall.

The floor-through hall, RIGHT, *is accentuated by two long painted-wood tabletops set on huge tree trunks, with equally massive log baskets beneath. Up the staircase is a series of 24 engravings of Indian scenes dating between 1795 and 1797.* LEFT, In *the country, a man may wear many hats.*

Fine lace curtains allow the sun to stream into the southwest-facing
drawing room. Simple cotton slipcovers are softened by chintz-covered cushions.
On the walls above the sofa is a collection of 19th- and 20th-century
painters including James Lloyd. The Georgian ceiling and door
moldings give definition to this comfortable room. The glass screen in
front of the fireplace contains stuffed birds and butterflies.

A *writing desk,* LEFT, *with poppies and buttercups and a view of green fields. The fabric of the festoon blind is from David Ison.*

The *red drawing room,* ABOVE, *has subtle decorative effects: green piping for the red slipcovers, three-quarter-height bookshelves, mirror lining the sides of the bookshelves and inset in the paneled doors that lead into the conservatory. The elaborate picture arrangement over the fireplace, mostly of cottages and landscapes, is dominated by a portrait of an Edwardian lady by the American artist Charles Shannon.*

Through the glass doors, one enters the conservatory, RIGHT, added to the house in 1889. It boasts two chandeliers, interesting ornaments, and plants chosen for their scent—geraniums, white jasmine, gardenia.

The upstairs landing, ABOVE, *a brilliant blue with a touch of Chinese Chippendale, elaborate Georgian over-door moldings, and rush matting. On the walls are paintings by John Piper. In the foreground, baskets of laundry belonging to the children—with labels.*

Violets are the theme, BELOW, *for the bedroom of one of the family's five children, decorating a canopied bed, tablecloths, and armchair. A ceiling frieze adds architectural interest.*

Another child's room, RIGHT, *this time with a white wrought-iron bed, cotton spread, chintz cushions, and an eclectic picture collection (including a poem by grandfather).*

The master bath, LEFT, masculine in feel, thanks to the small brown print wallpaper, paneled bath and basin, and huge mahogany wardrobe. Heavy brown velvet curtains and the large circular gilt mirror evoke Victorian splendor.

Color is muted in the master bedroom, ABOVE, dominated by an ornate Italian 18th-century gilt headboard, which contrasts with the plain pine chest and rush matting. Stenciling by Mary MacCarthy and fabric hand-printed by Mrs. Richard Smith add decorative detail.

165

As *in so many old English houses, the kitchen,* BELOW, *was once the backstairs and butler's pantry. A tinted-glass Venetian chandelier presides over a scrubbed pine table, rush chairs, a green linoleum floor, and marigold-yellow walls. The stenciled cupboard doors are by Mary MacCarthy. The series of watercolors of French provincial scenes is by a relative.*

Breakfast *in the garden,* RIGHT, *protected by a lattice roof and huge pots of daisies.*

The *kitchen garden,* FAR RIGHT, *laid out with paths and beds. (In its Victorian years, the house had seven gardeners.) The high wall conceals the house from the village. The owners sold a David Hockney drawing to pay for the tennis court,* FAR RIGHT. *Its backdrop of a fine 18th-century stable barn makes a change from Wimbledon.*

Harbledown, A Village Near Canterbury *by Jonathan Skelton (ca. 1735–1759).*

Park Landscape with Sheep
by George Barret, Sr.
(1728/32–1784).

THE WELL-TEMPERED

WATERCOLOR PAINTING IS perhaps the only art that the English can claim to have originated in their own country. This is not to say that continental artists did not work in this medium; Dürer, Holbein, Van Dyck, Rubens, and many other masters used watercolors. But the form was chosen largely for sketches, or for small cartoons in preparation for what was to be the serious, much larger scale opus—in oils.

One of the most famous early English watercolorists was Nicholas Hilliard, the miniaturist, who was born in 1537 and died in 1619, and who painted many of the great figures of his day. But the medium was difficult to use—artists had to prepare their own colors,

Purley Hall, Berkshire,
1756, *by Francis Cotes*
(1726–1770).

A Country House in a
Wooded Landscape *by*
Michael Angelo Rooker
(1746–1801).

WATERCOLOR

and the procedure for mixing the gum arabic (which bound the pigment to the paper) was both time-consuming and easily botched. Few artists then preferred watercolor to oil.

Seventeenth-century England saw the arrival of many distinguished Dutch artists, who traveled around the country and recorded what they saw in paint. The English took to this idea, and inspired by other Europeans such as Claude Lorraine, Nicolas Poussin, and Salvator Rosa—who painted European scenes that became so popular that their engravings were hung in many great houses—they invaded the Continent in droves, armed with a questing eye and a sketchbook.

The Gunpowder Magazine, Hyde Park
by Paul Sandby (1731–1809).

Bromley Hill, *1812, by Peter de Wint
(1784–1849).*

When they came back, like present-day tourists with their snapshots of the Parthenon, the English artists had a body of work to show their friends.

Landscape art reached its height in the 18th century, the century of romanticism. Contemplation of the landscape became more inward-looking, and as the Romantic movement swept the country, the English countryside became the source of all truth and beauty. Painters rushed to the Lake District, scoured their home counties, and traveled to out-of-the-way places to commune with Nature and their paintbrushes.

For these activities, watercolor was the perfect medium. By this time, thanks to the inventions of William and Thomas Reeves (who brought out ready-mixed paints) and, later, Winsor and Newton (who in the 1830s produced paint in tubes), one could go anywhere with one's trusty paint box. (These names are still seen on paint boxes today.) The paints were light and portable, and could be successfully used outdoors, on the spot, where Nature's light and rhythms should be recorded. The effects of watercolors, with their transparency and clarity, more closely resembled the artist's vision than the heavier, more formal impact of oils. The German observer Muthesius, on noting the English partiality to watercolors, said, "It is almost as though the overcast English sky were too dark for oil paintings, just as it has been responsible for the progressive lightening of English colored-glass windows."

Certainly, the artists themselves were aware of Nature's contribution to their art. John Sell Cotman (1782–1842), a brilliant and underrecognized watercolorist, wrote a letter describing having found the ideal day for an artist, in that it had "fine clouds, the shadows of which give life and spirit to everything, and change upon change takes place like magic, from light tones to deepest purples." And how many artists would bother to note the wind's direction in his description of a painting, as John Constable (1776–1837) does? "Study of Clouds Above a Wide Landscape: about 11—noon—Sepr 15 1830—Wind—W."

In the 18th century, architects such as William Kent, James Stuart, Robert Adam, and Christopher Wren had begun to produce art-quality watercolor renderings of the houses they designed, placing them meticulously in the landscape to which they so symbiotically belonged. Many of the painters who dominated the form during its peak period in the 19th century started out as draftsmen or topographers, who added color for interest to their architectural drawings and maps. Master watercolorists Thomas Girtin and J. M. W. Turner, for instance, both born in 1775, were trained as topographical draftsmen. Paul Sandby, another fine painter, was a military draftsman who graduated to landscapes and street scenes from camps and campaign plans. Even Gainsborough painted watercolor landscapes of his beloved Suffolk when he could get away from what he called "this curs'd Face Business."

The astonishing success of these artists, and the growing repute accorded their work, brought about the founding of the Royal Society of Painters in Water-Colours in 1804. The Royal Academy had been slow to recognize the authenticity of watercolor art. (It was not until 1943 that a watercolor artist was elected to associate membership.) In retaliation, the watercolorists created their own society. The first exhibition was mounted in 1805, with 275 paintings—all framed as grandly as the oil paintings shown by their rivals at the Royal Academy. The most expensive works were by Samuel Shelley and cost 26 pounds, 10 shillings, and sixpence.

The Shepherd: Evening, Buckinghamshire, *1845,* ABOVE, *by Francis Oliver Finch (1802–1862).*

A Yorkshire Road, LEFT, *by Peter de Wint.*

Bird's Nest with Sprays of Apple Blossoms, BELOW, *by William Henry Hunt (1790–1864).*

In Richmond Park *by John William Inchbold (1830–1888).*

The Great Parlour at Strawberry Hill *by John Carter.*

While professional artists were promoting their art, a new group was putting work on display. In the 19th century, it was considered de rigueur for young females not only to be accomplished pianists but also to show some skill with a paintbrush. Victorian family albums are filled with pictures of young ladies sketching in the garden, or in the Lake District, or in the Forum in Rome. Most country houses have on their walls mementos of a great-aunt's sketching skills. These were enjoyed not only for sentimental reasons but also because many middle-class families wanted to decorate their houses with something other than a six-foot-long portrait of an ancestor, stuffed in a huge gilded frame. Watercolors, both professional and amateur, were highly acceptable as ornament, sometimes three or four on top of each other, or packed like a jigsaw puzzle across a whole wall.

Very English, this. Other countries never developed the art of watercolors to the same extent. Indeed, in France it was not considered a legitimate art at all until a selection of British watercolors was shown at the Paris Salon of 1824—and caused a sensation. One reason, perhaps, for this singular lack of influence abroad is that during some of the busiest years of the watercolor artists —roughly between 1750 and 1830—England was involved in a series of wars against France, and was thus forced to be even more isolated and insular than usual.

While watercolors were becoming increasingly accepted at home as collectible art, a problem arose that almost caused the bottom to drop out of the market. It was discovered in the middle of the last century that daylight faded the pictures, so that they became "pale ghosts of their former selves," as the superintendent of the art collections at South Kensington Museum said. There was a big debate on the matter, involving many distraught collectors and artists in whose interest it was to deny any such diminishing of quality. But it was finally understood, after the dissemination of much scientific evidence, that light can indeed damage the color pigments in watercolor paintings, particularly in conjunction with erratic room temperatures. Twentieth-century museums and collectors are wise to hang their paintings in air-conditioned rooms with careful lighting.

Today, English watercolors are highly prized almost everywhere, including those by modern exponents such as Rex Whistler, John Piper, David Gentleman, the Nash brothers, and David Hockney. Yale University has one of the finest collections in the world, and prices in the auction houses rise yearly. Great-aunt Juliet's charming efforts, hanging modestly all these years in a country drawing room, are being eyed by their owners with an entirely new respect.

A Summer Day *by John Sell Cotman (1782–1842).*

The Amateur *by Frederick Walker (1840–1875).*

RASHLEIGHAYES

THIS WORKING FARM has its origins in the very earliest form of house building in England. Many Pre-Norman houses show a similar architecture—a one-storied rectangle with a long roof under which both animals and people took their shelter. Superior civilization through later centuries demanded the addition of second or third stories, and the separation of human beings from their livestock. "Long" houses can still be seen in Devonshire and in parts of Scotland, where the low roof line of barn and adjoining house nestle easily in the steep inclines of the mountainous surrounding countryside.

This modest house sits at the foot of a steep hill, with the slopes of the Dart Valley sweeping up behind it.

*Ingenuity on a masterly scale
—the Wellington boot as
hinged drainpipe. Its creator
"desperately needed a right
angle." Geraniums, lobelia, and
ivy spill out of neighboring urns.*

The back door, RIGHT,
*painted pink, with family boots
and dog.*

The farm has sheep and bullocks, at least three
dogs, at least four cats, and an uncountable
number of chickens. The interior is practical
rather than glamorous, as befits a family with
children and a typical farmer's budget. One
evening, the story goes, when one of the
children was newly born, the nurse, sitting in
the kitchen, heard the infant crying upstairs.

"How wonderful," she said. "You have
an intercom for the baby."

"Oh, no," said the father. "It's just a hole in the ceiling above the Aga."

The only concession to decorating came when the
owners found they needed more entertaining space. One
of the barns was commandeered and transformed, by their
own hands, into a high-ceilinged, airy drawing room.

The barn walls to the right of the farmhouse are
made of materials 400 years old, before the invention of
cement. Called "cob" (the west of England's word for
mud), the substance is a combination of soil, stone, and
water, all crushed together on the ground and churned
up by the feet of bullocks. This mixture is then poured
in between wooden planks and allowed to set. Cob walls
were often up to four feet thick, and took much time to
build, as each layer had to set before the next could be
added. Whitewash or a lime plaster was usually the last
step in finishing the job, often applied with tar in order
to deter animals from licking holes in the wall.

Cob continued to be used well into the 18th century, often with flint and thatch, since it provided a rustic
look and lasted unusually well, even in wet weather.
Other forms of unbaked earth, with which houses all over
England were built over 300 years ago, have mostly van-
ished from the countryside, but the cob cottages that have
survived in Devon, Somerset, and Cornwall continue to
give pleasure to those who discover them.

The exterior of the farm,
PREVIOUS PAGE, *showing
the back garden and to the left
the livestock barns, stocking
sheep and bullocks; and the
lush landscape of Devon,
famous for Sir Francis Drake
and clotted cream.*

The front of the house, BELOW, *with the original cob wall on the right (the red soil is typical of Devonshire) and the converted drawing room on the left. Inside the barn,* RIGHT, *are stalls for animals. Up high are the original roof beams of untreated bark.*

From barn, FAR RIGHT, *to drawing room. The same 16-foot ceiling, the same beams; everything else somewhat different. The walls are creamy ivory; the furniture is pine and mahogany; the sofa is slipcovered in corduroy.*

COUNTRY CRAFTS

THE FIRST ENGLISH country houses had thatched roofs, covering a timber-framed ceiling structure. Thatch was cheap, the materials, mostly reed and straw, were easy to find, and it gave good protection. For house walls built with soft materials, such as cob (a mixture of mud and stone), thatch was lighter and less likely to sink than slate or stone. It was, however, combustible, and a law was passed in 1212 that no thatch could be used on houses in London.

Although thatch tends to be connected with lowly dwellings, it was used on grander houses as well. Hammoon Manor, in Dorset, for instance, has a fine thatched roof. The house is named after William de Moion, who contributed 47 knights to the Battle of Hastings in 1066, at which the Saxon king, Harold, was defeated by the Normans. But as more sophisticated materials were introduced by foreigners—the Dutch bringing bricks and tiles in the 16th century and the French contributing corbel-supported turrets and classical details in the 17th—fashion as well as practicality dictated that thatch give way to less flammable and more hardy materials. By the 18th century, almost all new roofing was built with slate or tile.

In the 19th century, thatch had a renaissance, thanks to the fashion of the age for the "picturesque," rustic, and Gothic styles. *Cottages ornées* (like Sir Henry Hoare's folly near Stourhead) were built for rich patrons, made of thatch and stucco and surrounded by lush greenery, reflecting the current taste for historicism and

An ancient craft, beautifully rendered. To thatch this Dorset cottage will cost about $8,000, and it should last about 40 years. A fine example, RIGHT, *of thatch on a barn in Wiltshire.*

romance, as opposed to the severe classicism of the previous century. Whole villages were designed with this principle in mind, including Great Tew, in Oxfordshire, a time-warp vision of thatch and Gothic arches and creamy Cotswold stone, designed by the architect J. C. Loudon in the early 1800s. These revivals, plus the remnants of an older history, account for some of the 50,000 thatched cottages left in England.

Yet it is a living art, both for houses and barns, particularly in the south of England where the climate is more temperate. There are 50 thatchers in Dorset alone, and good thatching jobs may be found in Dorset, Devon, and Sussex. In the old days, thatch was supposed to last one hundred years. Today, the thatcher of an average Dorset cottage estimates his roof will last only about forty years. He uses water reeds, which are harvested and baled. The bales are then laid on the roof with iron pegs and wooden staples, and batted into shape. The reeds are never, ever cut. Even the intricate scalloped edging is done by skillful alignment of the reed tips, rather than by snipping the ends. The results of these skills, harking back centuries, invoke a sense of warmth and shelter in the most modest of dwellings as well as the grandest of follies.

MAKING WHEELS BY hand is also a rare craft these days, yet the wagon is still a familiar sight on the estate of many country houses in England. There are only about fifty wheelwrights left in England, compared to over four hundred in Lincolnshire alone at the turn of the century. Wheelwrights today make much of their living making wheels for 19th-century wagons, either for use by farmers or for museums and shows. The wheel is all dry-jointed—no glue or nails. It must be planed to a perfect curve by hand. This is a craft, like thatch, that has been superseded by modern technology.

A *farm wagon,* ABOVE, *from the collection at Littlecote House, in Berkshire, with wheels made by a craftsman like Peter Small. The cart horse being shod in the Littlecote stables,* BELOW, *is also part of an old tradition.*

THE BLACKSMITH, ON the other hand, is as vital to English country life as he ever was. The word comes from the fact that this craftsman works in black metal such as iron, as opposed to a "whitesmith," who works in tin or silver. Much mythology has been built up around the smithy, or rather the artifact it produces, the horseshoe. Widely regarded as a lucky charm, or amulet, horseshoes are frequently to be seen tacked onto walls or doors of houses to ward off the Evil Eye, or to discourage witchcraft.

Nobody has yet invented a better way to shoe a horse, and blacksmiths today travel 20,000 miles a year to work on their clients' racehorses, jumpers, hunters, and children's ponies. In earlier times, the horse came to the blacksmith. Now, the smithy is mobile, thanks to portable gas tanks, which provide heat for the anvil. For many English, however, in spite of modern science, Henry Wadsworth Longfellow's well-known poem about the village blacksmith evokes the best image of this indispensable craftsman:

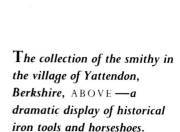

The collection of the smithy in the village of Yattendon, Berkshire, ABOVE —*a dramatic display of historical iron tools and horseshoes.*

Robert Hall, LEFT, *blacksmith, shoeing Meg at Hovington House in Wiltshire.*

> Under the spreading chestnut tree,
> The village smithy stands;
> The smith, a mighty man is he,
> With large and sinewy hands;
> And the muscles of his brawny arms
> Are strong as iron bands.
>
> Week in, week out, from morn till night,
> You can hear his bellows blow;
> You can hear him swing his heavy sledge,
> With measured beat and slow,
> Like a sexton ringing the village bell,
> When the evening sun is low.

STOURPAINE

MUCH OF THE land in this part of Dorset was owned
for generations by the Portman family. This house, dating from the period of Queen Anne (1702–1714), came
into prominence later in the 18th century when two
Portman sisters, who unfortunately failed to marry, were
"banished" from the family's more fashionable residence
across the river at Durweston and sent to live out
their lives in this form of dower house. (Strictly speaking, a dower house is one belonging to a deceased
husband's estate in which the law allows his widow to
live for life. Hence, also, the word *dowager*.) For the two
Portman spinsters, an extension was added—the Georgian
side. At different times in its later history, the house has
been both a private home and a school. The present owner
inherited the house from his parents, and now lives here

The drawing room, LEFT, has unmatched loose cotton slipcovered sofas and chairs, an embroidered silk Indian coverlet on the coffee table, and lace, velvet, and patchwork cushions. A kilim rug covers beige matting on the floor. The lamp bases are Indian tea caddies. The portrait is of a Neapolitan woman by Jacqueline Comerre-Paton. The wonderfully casual flower arrangement, ABOVE, includes alchemilla, foxglove, and salvia.

The noble Georgian facade of Stourpaine, PREVIOUS PAGE, framed by the Dorset hills, looks out on a lawn, gardens, and a fine old spruce tree. The original entrance of the house, which is hidden by a high wall, is at the side, facing the village street.

with his wife and three children. An unpretentious family house, it sits in a walled garden, totally concealed from the road, yet within walking distance of village shops.

The entertaining rooms are Georgian in proportion, with big south-facing windows reaching to the floor, and finely molded fireplaces. The staircase is the oldest element of the house, a charming circular affair, so tucked into the architecture that it is impossible to photograph. Upstairs, the Georgian bedrooms contrast with the older, smaller rooms assigned to children.

The decorating in the downstairs rooms has an Indian flavor, thanks to the collection of Indian artifacts inherited by great-grandmothers and parents. Throughout the house are signs of international travel, as well as more traditional English objects. The walls in the drawing room and dining room (formerly two rooms, but now joined by means of a wide opening) are painted a glowing apricot, the effect achieved by a mixture of stipple work and scumble glaze (a dark over a lighter wash).

Outside, there are a kitchen garden and a formal front garden with croquet lawn, defined by a long, low brick wall, staircase, and decorative urns. A covered walkway leads from the village gate to the original Queen Anne entrance, enhanced by clematis, violas, lobelia, and pink roses.

189

The apricot of the drawing room is carried through into the dining room.
The heavy white cotton swagged curtains with ornate gilt pelmets also
continue the drawing room theme. On the table, a blue embroidered cloth from
Damascus covers green baize, with more of the flowery china hat collection.
Mahogany furniture, a large gilt mirror, a pair of gilt candelabra, and
Victorian marble busts give weight to this elegant room.

This china hat containing flowers, LEFT, is one of
many collected and decorated by the lady of the house.

The upstairs landing of an English country house, ABOVE,
often affords the opportunity for a pleasing decorative arrangement.
Here a sofa is slipcovered in cotton ticking. The two statues are
wooden frogs brought back from Bali. Through the window, a view
of the kitchen garden.

This spare bedroom, in the older part of the house, has an attic roof,
a small floral wallpaper, lace covers over pink-and-white
gingham eiderdowns, and Colefax & Fowler honeysuckle chintz
curtains and bed ruffle.

POTTERY
POTPOURRI

WE THINK OF Egyptians and Greeks when we think of pottery. We think of the Chinese when we think of porcelain. We don't think of the English in this context much at all until the end of the 17th century, which is as it should be, since the English seem to have coasted through the Middle Ages with better architecture than art and better politics than pots.

What galvanized the English ceramic makers into action was one of those sociological problems, like the weather, which demands new solutions from artists and artisans. (The cold weather, for instance, induced northern countries to invent the eiderdown.) It was the introduction of hot drinks such as tea and coffee into England during the reign of the Stuart kings, as a chic alternative to the traditional cold beverages such as wine and ale, that forced potters to produce containers able to withstand the heat, and thus a new industry was born.

Ceramic factories began to produce vast quantities of vessels, mostly lead-glazed or salt-glazed, sometimes decorated with incised designs filled with blue coloring (known as "scratch blue") or with applied reliefs of

China belonging to the Sykes family displayed in a cabinet in Sledmere House, Yorkshire. The blue-and-white armorial china is 18th-century Chinese pottery.

On the base of each piece of the Sykes armorial china is the owner's mark, Triton, son of Neptune. The Chinese craftsmen, however, mistakenly rendered the god as a mermaid. (When a Scottish family commissioned some Chinese porcelain in the 19th century, the family motto, "Unite," was to be inscribed on the service. When it arrived from China, the inscription read, "Untie.")

195

Sledmere china, with coat of arms and decoration.

flowers and animals. Later different types of stoneware were introduced, and in 1813 Charles James Mason patented Ironstone china, a tough mixture of ironstone slag mixed with porcelain, which was one of the hardest materials of all the pottery types, and much used for everyday household needs.

The industry was centered around Stoke-on-Trent, and the other Five Towns immortalized by Arnold Bennett, in the county of Staffordshire. The reason for its location in this otherwise unprepossessing part of the Midlands is twofold. First, during the late 17th and 18th centuries, forested land was being increasingly absorbed for agricultural use, thus making brushwood, which was used for firing kilns, prohibitively expensive. Staffordshire produced not only good-quality clay but also coal, which was found to be an excellent substitute for wood. Second, the county was one of the few areas of England without huge private estates. Proof of this can be seen today, in that Staffordshire can boast only 5 major stately houses in the National Trust directory, compared to 14 in Cheshire and 16 in Buckinghamshire, counties of comparable size. Since the land was divided into groups of smallholdings, rather than vast tracts of private property, the potters could all work at their craft on their own small properties, which they owned rather than rented.

When people think of English pottery, Staffordshire comes immediately to mind, and in particular the series of figures that began to appear in the 18th century. They were made out of fairly rough dark-brown or beige clay and then covered with a yellowish lead glaze. Designed for the local market, the figures usually represented familiar characters—gamekeepers, fiddlers, soldiers, shepherds, dogs. Later the sculpting and colors became more subtle and sophisticated, with rich greens, purples, and blues enhancing the lifelike statuettes. The work of

Sledmere china hung on a wall in the dining room.

Ralph Wood and his son, exponents of this art, has been compared to that of Hogarth in its depiction of English working-class life.

The Staffordshire potters also had an eye to the export market, both in Europe and in America. William Ridgway and Company, for instance, produced painted scenes of romanticized European landscapes on their plates and dishes, appealing particularly to the American taste. They also produced American scenes, painted by William Henry Bartlett, then transfer-printed. ("Villa on the Hudson" was the sort of title.) Ridgway and Company was also one of many pottery firms making inexpensive blue-and-white stoneware, known in the United States as flow blue. By the 19th century, huge amounts of Staffordshire pottery were crossing the Atlantic. A single shipment from Enoch Wood & Sons to a china broker in Philadelphia contained 262,000 pieces.

Dessert dish with shell-molded handles, 1811–1820.

Meat dish, "Mason's Oak," depicting a pastoral scene.

A *Mason's Ironstone teapot and stand, 1805–1810,* ABOVE *and* BELOW.

A *family collection, of blue-and-white Chinese export china.*

White *jug, molded in relief, about 1825.*

Dessert dish with shell-shaped handle, about 1820.

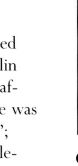

Gold-decorated meat dish depicting Holyrood Palace.

Gold decoration surrounds this picture of Belvoir Castle.

Sometimes the potters might get slightly carried away with their American success. Benjamin Franklin was honored with a model made of himself by a Staffordshire artist when he was in England. This figure was marketed under three names: first, as "B. Franklin"; then, to broaden the appeal, "English country gentleman"; and finally, for good measure, since nobody in Europe knew what he looked like, "G. Washington."

Apart from these decorative figures, English pottery was originally for use rather than for ornament, and most of the surviving examples are of a practical nature. Josiah Wedgwood, patriarch of English china, was the first to institute mass production for his dishes, jugs, and plates, introducing standardized shapes by means of mechanical methods that changed the face of the industry. The other dramatic innovation, and one that changed the course of Staffordshire's history, was the discovery of porcelain.

The Chinese (and after them, the Japanese) had been making porcelain for hundreds of years, but the secret remained in the East. Porcelain was fired at much higher temperatures, and was translucent when held up to the light, as opposed to earthenware, delft, or majolica. Its appeal to the Europeans, apart from its lightness and delicacy, lay in its whiteness (compared to the less attractive earth tones of pottery) and its ability to withstand heat. The major European porcelain makers in the 16th and 17th centuries were Dresden (Meissen) and Sèvres. England entered the lists officially in 1745, with the Chelsea factory producing the first-known examples.

There were two ways of making porcelain. Hard paste, the Chinese way, was a mixture of china clay (kaolin) and china rock (petuntze). The Europeans, particularly the English, went for soft paste, which was made with clay, ground glass, and crushed bone ash, and other combinations. Bone ash was first used at the Bow

Mason's Ironstone Sandringham plate—one of a series of six plates produced to celebrate Christmas.

Colorful Mason's Ironstone plates, ABOVE and BELOW, with typical floral design, dating from the mid-19th century.

factories, near London. (Some of the clay in Bow came from North Carolina, where good-quality kaolin had been discovered in 1739.) Spode, in Staffordshire, produced what came to be called bone china in the 1790s, using this new mixture of calcined animal bones, clay, and stone, and from then on, English porcelain became known as bone china throughout the world.

Many of these manufacturers were based in other places as well as Staffordshire, and were privately run businesses, unlike in Europe, where porcelain makers were often under the patronage of kings or ducal palaces. The English court and aristocrats certainly commissioned works to celebrate themselves but there are few collections comparable to Marie Antoinette's Sèvres, for instance.

Thanks to the increasing popularity of tea, coffee, and bonbons after dessert, the manufacturers did a good business turning out teapots, coffeepots, sugar bowls, creamers, and the other paraphernalia of an elegant "at home." Josiah Wedgwood, perhaps the most brilliant of all the porcelain makers, also began producing other kinds of domestic wares. Before the 18th century, for instance, people customarily ate off communal plates. Wedgwood and his colleagues introduced individual plates and dishes for a reasonable price, and suddenly everyone was expecting his own place setting for dinner.

The more refined colors and designs that could be used on porcelain dealt a heavy blow to the potteries. Some quickly started producing porcelain themselves; others closed down. Pottery never recovered its position as the prime source of vessels for the home, but many pieces of Staffordshire, Leeds, Liverpool (where delft ware was produced), Castleford, and Ferrybridge are still to be admired for their fine shapes and colors, the results of some unknown potter's skill.

Four more Staffordshire plates, showing scenes from rural life. A family of copper luster dogs, LEFT, favorites of Staffordshire collectors.

Shelves of Staffordshire jugs, cachepots, tankards, and vases, ABOVE. *Staffordshire plates and jugs,* BELOW, *dated 1879 and 1883, and in the center The Trojan Lion.*

A *Staffordshire menagerie,* ABOVE, *with alphabet and hunting mugs. An unusual piece—a cow holding up a container declaring "Pure Milk,"* BELOW.

BIDDESDEN

FOR SOME VIVID vignettes of English life one could hardly do better than acquaint oneself with the history of Biddesden, a house lovingly documented since its earliest incarnation. A fine example of early 18th-century architecture, it was built in 1711 by General Webb, one of the Duke of Marlborough's military colleagues, who gained some notoriety for complaining that his successful siege against the French at Wynendael was wrongly attributed to Major General Cadogan (one of Marlborough's favorites) instead of to Webb himself. Whatever the truth of this misunderstanding (which was later taken up by Thackeray, a relative of the Webb family), the general was

The east side of the brick and stone house, ABOVE, shows the tower, built by General Webb to house the bell he was awarded for his exploits in battle. Three ground-floor windows have been amusingly painted in trompe l'oeil, PREVIOUS PAGE, during Biddesden's current ownership —one by Lytton Strachey's devoted friend Dora Carrington and the other two by Roland Pym.

The west side of Biddesden, RIGHT and FAR RIGHT, looks out on gardens and wild flowers, where a path has been cut to make a pleasing vista.

Through this archway, FAR LEFT, a flagstone pathway leads to the door of the pool pavilion. Another archway, LEFT, reveals a mini-garden and thatched wall of the pool pavilion.

rewarded for his efforts with the gift of a large bell, cast in 1660, for which he built the clock tower at Biddesden. The exterior of the house undoubtedly reflects in other ways the self-esteem of its first owner.

The house changed hands very few times in the intervening centuries, and was bought in 1931 by Bryan Guinness (now Lord Moyne), the poet and author, who was then married to one of the famous Mitford sisters, Diana (later Lady Mosley). Biddesden thus became a center for painters, poets, and artists of the 1930s, and in particular a home-away-from-home for Lytton Strachey, who lived nearby at Hamspray. Strachey's loving friend Dora Carrington painted one of the trompe l'oeil windows at the side of the house. (After Strachey's death, Bryan Guinness used to invite Carrington for pony trap rides around Biddesden, but she could not be consoled and killed herself soon after.)

Another contemporary, the architect George Kennedy, designed for the Guinnesses a gazebo and swimming pool, with mosaics by Boris Anrep. Kennedy also landscaped some of the gardens, with statues and allées.

After his divorce from Diana Mitford, Bryan Guinness married Elisabeth Nelson in 1936, and added nine more children to the two sons from his first marriage, many of whom still live in or around Biddesden. The house thus became essentially a family house, with all the accoutrements that such a role entails.

Lord Moyne wrote in his book *Potpourri from the Thirties,* "To me a home in the country was a gateway to happiness." This feeling permeates Biddesden. "My roots and my family's," wrote the author, "have gone deeply into the fields and woods which the General must have owned in the 18th Century." There is a legend that if the portrait of General Webb that hangs in the hall is ever removed from Biddesden, his ghost will haunt the house forever after. No one so far has volunteered to test the story.

The magnificent hall, RIGHT, *is dominated by the haunted portrait of General Webb, builder of Biddesden. The carved fireplace is Georgian, the fine 17th-century Brussels tapestries are by Reydams, the painted cabinet is English. The left-hand doorway leads to the staircase.*

Going up the stairs, BELOW, *the visitor is greeted by a beautiful Georgian banister and a portrait of society hostess Mrs. Willett, by George Romney.*

The long, light drawing room, LEFT, has fine 18th-century paneling, moldings, and fireplace. Unmatched chairs surround the table, where Lord Moyne and his daughter are having tea. Pink-and-white chintz slipcovers and exuberant flower arrangements give a feeling of comfort and informality to this grandly proportioned room. Detail of the far end of the room, ABOVE, showing the collection of English bone china in coral-lined display shelves.

The kitchen at Biddesden, ABOVE, *is large enough to cope*
with the many mouths it must provide food for. Three separate work
surfaces or tables sit quite comfortably in the space, with generous storage
and a large pantry through the open doorway.

Twenty *for dinner is par for the course here on weekends. The large*
painting on the right is by Stanley Spencer, and a portrait by Gainsborough
hangs over the fireplace. The chair covers have an unusual classical motif.

The stables of Biddesden, LEFT, *are built in the same mellow brick as the house and decorated with climbers and flower beds.*

The poultry may be normal, *but some of the birds in the dovecotes,* BELOW, *most assuredly are not. They are called tumbler pigeons, a rare and eccentric breed that with the encouragement of sharp claps of the hand will fly up in the air and turn somersaults.*

Rows of apple trees, RIGHT, grow out of luxuriant beds of polyanthus.

Steps from the croquet lawn, OVERLEAF, are planted with forget-me-nots, frankenia, veronica, dianthus, campanula, erinus, phlox, hebe, and creeping jenny.

Untrustworthy topiary buttresses "support" the walls that separate the gardens from the swimming pool. Between each buttress a miniature garden is planted, with wisteria, climbing roses, foxglove, columbine, and poppies.

216

218

THIS SPORTING LIFE

WHO INVENTED FOX hunting? The idea of chasing over the countryside on horseback after a prey that is never intended to be eaten, but is simply dismembered may seem the height of decadence, but it has remained the premier sport for English country dwellers since the 17th century. The national passion for horses and dogs finds its apotheosis in fox hunting, an exhilarating combination of speed, skill, and blood in which both men and women can become equally proficient. ("Women never look so well as when one comes in wet and dirty from hunting," wrote that 19th-century Homer of the hunting field, R. S. Surtees.)

A *huntsman summons his hounds to action at the start of the day's sport.*

The country is divided up into hunt "countries"— the Pytchley, the Quorn, the Heythrop, the Cottesmore, the Grafton, the Middleton, the Belvoir, and so on. About 100,000 people in Britain and Ireland ride regularly to hounds. There are 446 hunts and 237 packs of foxhounds currently in action, so the foxes are kept busy. Each hunt has a Master of Foxhounds, a title regarded by some as more distinguished than that of Prime Minister, the MFH after your name valued more highly than the OBE. The meet is his great moment, for he is in command of the hounds, the hunt servants, and, more important, the followers, who must obey his orders.

Biddesden, like many country houses, is sometimes the venue for a meet, providing a glorious setting for the local hunt here gathering in the early morning.

219

"The English country gentleman
galloping after a fox—
the unspeakable in full pursuit
of the uneatable."
OSCAR WILDE

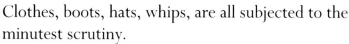

Hunting etiquette is as elaborate as the ceremony governing a visit to Buckingham Palace. Woe betide the poor novice who makes some blunder on the field. Clothes, boots, hats, whips, are all subjected to the minutest scrutiny.

An important ritual in hunting is to be "bloodied" (smeared with the fox's blood), which indicates that one has lasted the course, shown courage, and witnessed one's first kill. Children's stories abound of young heroes and heroines riding to hounds, yearning for and yet fearful of this traditional accolade. Without it, you might as well retire to the nursery and a seat on your rockinghorse.

Between the wars at Badminton, the Beaufort estate in Avon, the fox-hunting season started in August and continued until May, six days a week. The Beauforts owned 100 horses, with their own blacksmith and a groom to every two or three animals. The hunt had a huntsman and two whippers-in (who were in charge of the hounds). "We would get off very early in the morning," remembered the late Duke of Beaufort, "because one was out on a horse by half-past six."

Such keenness, exhibited by a people not given to an overabundance of emotion, is typical of the feeling fox hunting arouses in the English breast. "If we have it not, we die," wrote Surtees. "It's the sport of kings, the image of war without its guilt, and only five-and-twenty percent of its danger." This is the sort of overwrought prose fox hunting provokes. It also drives artists to hitherto un-scaled heights of inspiration. No self-respecting country house in England lacks at least one print, oil painting, or watercolor depicting a hunt—preferably a whole series. Titles such as *The Finest View in Europe* (the hunt as viewed from the seat of a horse) or *Tally Ho! Drawing the Spinney* (as a pack of hounds looks for a fox's scent) confirm the

excesses of artistic expression. The 18th-century artist James Ward, in his picture *Ralph Lampton and His Hounds,* lovingly painted in the name of every hound—Stormer, Lasher, Challenger, Huntsman, Rapid, etc.

In spite of increasing pressure being brought to bear from "anti-blood" sport groups (sometimes arousing quite unseemly behavior on both sides), this most English of passions refuses to abate. There is no better description of its attractions than in Nancy Mitford's novel *The Pursuit of Love:*

The next day, we all went out hunting. The Radletts loved animals, they loved foxes, they risked dreadful beatings to unstop their earths, they read and cried and rejoiced over Reynard the Fox, in summer they got up at four to go and see the cubs playing in the pale-green light of the woods; nevertheless, more than anything in the world they loved hunting. It was in their blood and bones and in my blood and bones, and nothing could eradicate it, though we knew it for a kind of original sin. For three hours that day I forgot everything except my body and my pony's body; the rushing, the scrambling, the splashing, struggling up the hills, sliding down them again, the tugging, the bucketing, the earth and the sky. I forgot everything, I could hardly have told you my name. That must be the hold that hunting has over people, especially stupid people; it enforces an absolute concentration, both mental and physical.

DODDINGTON HALL

DODDINGTON HALL WAS designed by Robert
Smythson, the great Elizabethan architect who produced
Wollaton Hall and Hardwick Hall, two of the greatest
English houses in the north of England. His employer was
Thomas Tailor, registrar to the Bishop of Lincoln. The
house was finished by 1600, and today looks almost
exactly as it did when the first owner took up residence.

    It is an Elizabethan house in the grand manner,
reflecting the characteristic Elizabethan values of confi-
dence and prosperity. Its foursquare, outward-facing
layout, its many windows, and its impressive symmetry

speak volumes about its period. Yet its simple, unadorned appearance (brick and quoin with very little ornament) reflects the flat, austere countryside of this part of north-eastern England, and the Dutch-gabled gatehouse is perhaps the only fanciful aspect of its architecture.

The Hussey family inherited the house from the Tailors, and through them the Delavals, Sir John Delaval being largely responsible for the 18th-century redecoration of the interior of the house. With his builders, the Lumby Brothers of Lincoln, Sir John introduced fine 18th-century plasterwork, and added paneling to counteract what he regarded as an excessive Elizabethan passion for windows. Sir John also installed double glazing in some of the bedrooms in order to overcome the drafts —the earliest known use of the technique. After various Delaval family exchanges in the late 18th century, George Ralph Payne Jarvis came to own Doddington in 1825 through a romantic attachment to Sarah Delaval Gunman, who, unlike poor Vita Sackville-West, was able to inherit Doddington since it was free of male entail. The lady died young and left the great house to her fortunate lover. The Jarvis family has lived at Doddington ever since. The present Jarvises, Antony and Vicky, have dedicated themselves to preserving the house and garden, both of which needed considerable help when they inherited it in 1973. Trained as an architect and agricultural scientist, Antony Jarvis was the ideal person to understand the house and its grounds, and both have greatly benefited from his expertise.

The house is full of furniture and collections that have been passed on through four centuries of continuous habitation without a change in family ownership. Portraits of Husseys and Delavals fill the Long Gallery, where Elizabethans were accustomed to exhibit their family pictures. Doddington's Long Gallery is a particularly fine example. It runs 96 feet between the two flanking wings

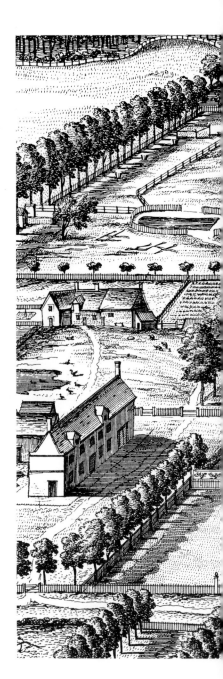

A *glimpse of iris, lupin, rose, and honeysuckle,* PREVIOUS PAGE, *these 18th-century Italian iron gates, set into high stone pillars with plinths, enclose the west garden of Doddington Hall. The portrait of Sarah Hussey by Kneller, from the white hall, was extended in Georgian times to fit the Georgian paneling installed by Sir John Delaval.*

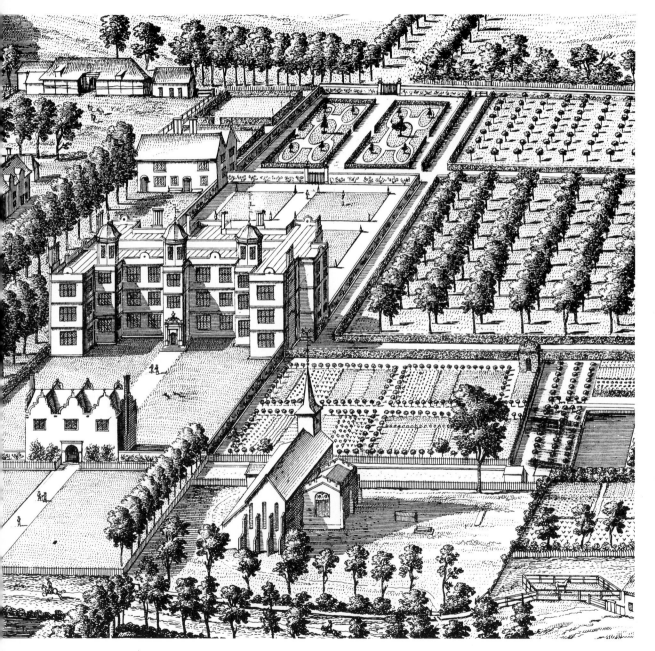

The gatehouse and the large walled kitchen garden, ABOVE LEFT, can be seen from the roof, and beyond it a field of yellow rape (so bright that an old curmudgeon once wrote to the London Times complaining that its color ruined the landscape).

A tapestry of Doddington Hall, ABOVE CENTER, made by local seamstress Margaret Smitten.

Doddington's croquet lawn, ABOVE. Croquet was always a popular sport for women. It is said that the crinoline was responsible for many triumphs, the huge skirt concealing convenient "adjustments" to the position of the ball. Beyond the croquet lawn is St. Peter's church, Norman in origin but rebuilt in 1775 in the Gothic style by the same Lumby who helped Sir John Delaval redecorate Doddington.

A 1707 engraving of Doddington Hall, LEFT, by Kip, shows Robert Smythson's symmetrical plan of two wings joined by a central hall.

229

The floor and fireplace of Doddington's original kitchen were raised to introduce light into what is now the Jarvises' private sitting room. The balcony was inspired by a trip to Amsterdam and was made by a local carpenter out of one of Doddington's walnut trees.

Decanters, glasses, dishes, bowls, jugs, and lampshades, collected over centuries.

A corner of the Jarvises' private hall, with a Dutch school painting over the table, Redouté roses on its left, tulips by 1920s artist Leonard Philpot on its right.

His master's voice—row of early Georgian servant's bells, with the name of each room inscribed beneath. Hand-painted stencils by Felicity Binyon and Elizabeth Macfarlane.

231

In this spare bedroom, LEFT, the walls are covered in an original William Morris willow pattern. The blue-and-white chintz is copied from a French toile. Above the fireplace is a portrait of the Jarvis family painted in the 1940s by the Viennese Secessionist artist M. Oppenheim.

of the house, with windows originally on both sides, the ones on the east side later bricked up by John Delaval in order to display his pictures. The Elizabethans used the gallery for recreation, lessons, and art; and as late as 1756 there is a record of the room being used for "a bowling alley."

Doddington has one of the oldest gardens in England, and following a 1707 engraving of the gardens, the Jarvises have worked devotedly to restore much of it to its ancient splendor. Formal in style, it reflects the taste of the owners. "A big square house," says Mr. Jarvis, "needs the feeling of having its feet firmly planted on the ground." Luckily for Doddington, even after 400 years, stability reigns.

Many of Doddington's historic rooms are open to the public. The interiors are in the private quarters belonging to the family, showing a more personal and less formal aspect than those seen on the house tour.

The south-facing master bedroom, its lightness accentuated by scrubbed pine furniture. The four-poster bed is decorated in Indian cotton fabric, the stripes used horizontally in order to diminish the height of the room.

In Doddington's attic, OVERLEAF, an invaluable storehouse of paintings and discarded heirlooms, as well as the famous "antler wall"—a unique display of irreplaceable nonsense, from old farm equipment to World War I gas masks.

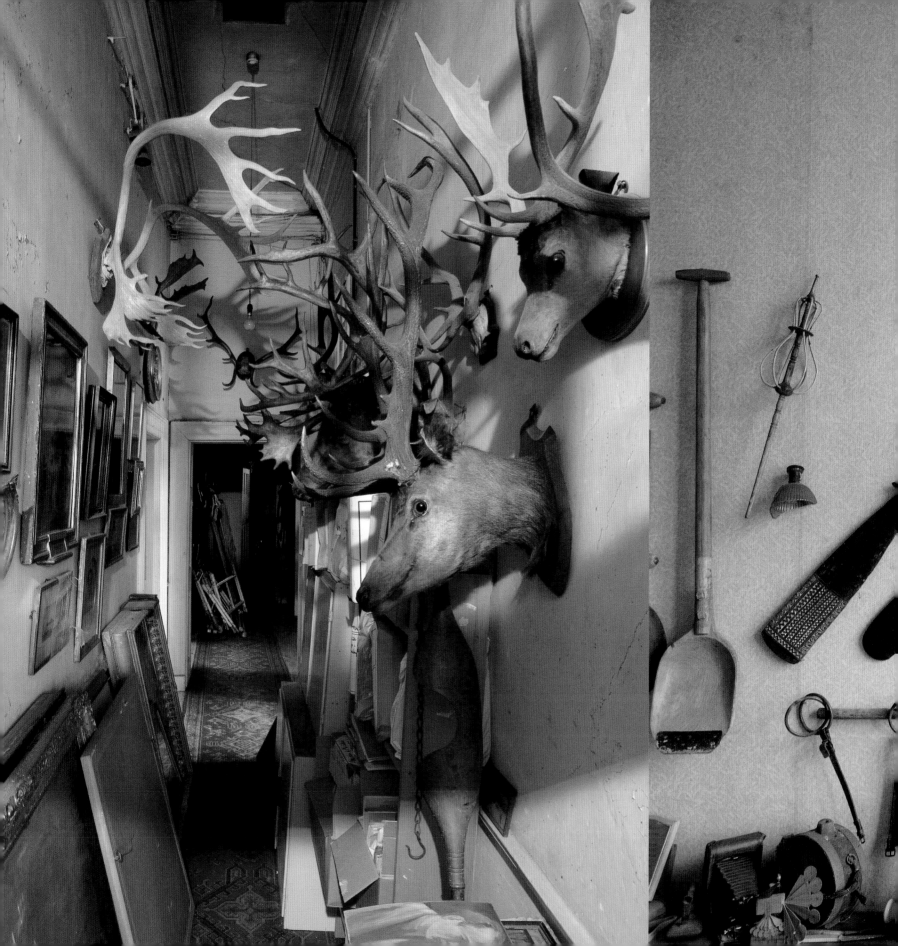

CLIMBING THE WALLS

IN THE EARLIEST medieval houses, wallpaper would have made no sense, since the walls were half-timbered, with uneven plasterwork—just the conditions to drive your local paperhanger to a nervous breakdown. Paneling was the best solution for irregular walls, since the panels, being fitted loosely, were flexible and could conceal the shape of the wall. The wood used was generally oak, being strong enough to withstand damp and rot. Mahogany, the wood one tends to associate with English country houses, is said to have been discovered in South America in 1597 by a carpenter on board one of Sir Walter Raleigh's ships, and was not in common use until the early 18th century.

Wainscoting, a form of paneling made with long planks laid like vertical clapboard, then tongued and grooved, was another way out of the irregular wall problem. It is mentioned as early as 1239, in an instruction from King Henry III to the Bailiff of Windsor, and in 1253 the king ordered "two hundred Norway boards of fir to wainscot therewith the chamber of our beloved son Edward in our castle of Winchester." This shows that fir was used in wainscoting, although the word *wainscot* was a medieval term for a high-quality oak imported from the Continent. The term is thought to have been connected to *wain,* meaning "wagon," for which this sturdy wood was also used. It is from this

By the time this woodblock-printed wallpaper, LEFT, *was in use about 1765, a tax had been imposed upon wallpaper production, greatly increasing its cost. A 19th-century wallpaper,* RIGHT, *showing the influence of Italian landscape painters and John Baptist Jackson.*

Frieze, about 1820, ABOVE, with a striking vine theme in relief.

An unused length of bamboo wallpaper, LEFT, border commissioned for the Royal Pavilion, Brighton, in the 1820s.

One of many examples of the strong Chinese influence, RIGHT, in wallpaper design in England—this one dated about 1850.

An example of flock, this border, ABOVE, has a band of horse chestnut leaves over a strip of olive-green flocking. Another pattern in flock, BELOW, showing its rich textural quality, dating about 1860.

form of wall paneling that the famous "linenfold" carving emerged, in which the panels look like draped fabric.

The wall decorations favored by those who could afford them were tapestries, usually made of woven wool or silk, or heavy silk or velvet hangings, which concealed a multitude of wall-surface sins, provided some form of insulation, and could also be moved from one house to another. Often highly colored and depicting vivid tableaux, from hunting scenes to heraldic displays, these were the forerunners of designer wallpaper.

With the disappearance of oak beams in the late Tudor period, it was possible to cover walls from floor to ceiling with plaster, which was then generally painted or stenciled. These were the walls on which Elizabethans loved to hang their paintings. A black-and-white wallpaper has been discovered dating from 1509, but sheets of decorated paper were also being used to line boxes and bind books, and their use for covering walls only really caught on in the 17th century. The early examples were offered as an alternative to the expensive fabric hangings found in the richer houses. Patterns were hand-printed on sheets, then pasted together for hanging on the wall. Flock paper, an invention of the English during the 17th century, consisted of the designs being printed with an adhesive, which were then dusted with fine sheep's wool, to imitate the

Peacocks and poppies and vibrant colors, RIGHT, mark the influence of the Arts and Crafts movement on wallpaper design.

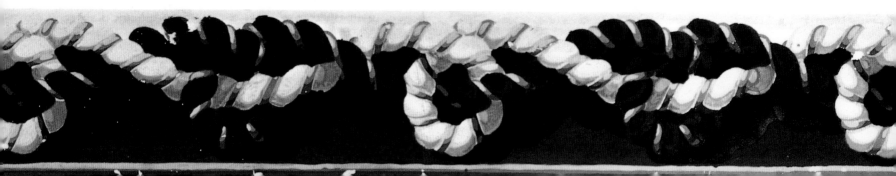

luxurious appearance of fabric on the wall.

As the Indo-European trade flourished, elegant Chinese wallpapers made their appearance in England, with colorful designs often in gold leaf or "teapaper," which became fashionable but prohibitively expensive. "I had heard of the fame of paper hangings and had some thought of sending for a suite," Lady Mary Wortley Montague wrote to her daughter in 1749, "but was informed that they were as dear as damask is here, which put an end to my curiosity." Thomas Chippendale was evidently undeterred (or working for a client who could afford it, Sir Rowland Winn), for at about the same time he was using Chinese wallpapers as the inspiration for a room in Nostell Priory in Yorkshire to set off his chinoiserie-style lacquered furniture that filled the house.

Part of the expense came from a tax which had been imposed on the sale of all wallpapers in 1712. By 1714, each sheet of paper that was intended to be painted or decorated had to be given an excise stamp and the tax of one and a half pennies paid to the Crown. This wallpaper duty priced many people out of the market, and until the tax was repealed in 1860, wallpaper was accessible only to the very rich. The Rococo stucco and plasterwork exemplified by the creations of the Adam brothers and Chippendale, seen in many stately homes, were also out of bounds for many small country house owners. Interiors for the most part from 1715 to 1860 depended on a good paint job.

Perhaps the most famous wallpaper designer of this period, reflecting the landscape movement, was John Baptist Jackson, who printed in oil colors and produced designs of amazing dramatic and visual qualities, inspired by the painters he admired—among them Canaletto, Claude Lorrain, and Salvator Rosa. Landscapes, classical ruins, medieval towers, every kind of Gothic scene, were reproduced on his papers, including effects in stucco and

Single Stem, NEAR RIGHT, *one of the papers from William Morris's original woodblocks designed by J. H. Dearle. Nursery wallpaper,* FAR RIGHT ABOVE, *one of many designed by Walter Crane between 1875 and 1885. The Bower,* FAR RIGHT BELOW, *an 1898 design by William Morris showing the increasing intricacy and subtlety of his work.*

242

marble. He wrote a large book on his work, in which he modestly claims:

"By this way of printing Paper, the Inventor has contrived that the Lights and Shades shall be broad and bold, and give great relief to the Figures; the finest Prints of all the antique Statues which imitate Drawings are introduced into Niches of Chiaro Oscuro in the Pannels of their Paper; these are surrounded with a Mosaic Work, in Imitation of Frames, or with Festoons and Garlands of Flowers, with great Elegance and Taste."

By the middle of the 19th century, it was possible to mass-produce papers by cylinder printing, and this development, along with the abolition of the prohibitive tax, meant that wallpaper became a common feature of English interiors. Thanks to William Morris, Walter Crane, C. L. Eastlake, C. F. A. Voysey, and others, the standard of design reached a peak in the second half of the 19th century, and many English country houses still boast wallpapers that were first produced during that time. Many of these artists' designs are still available today, as well as new ones produced by new techniques such as rotogravure and ink-embossed printing.

What makes wallpaper historians particularly happy is that in English houses it was never the custom, until well into this century, to remove the old wallpaper before pasting on a new one. Thus in some old houses as many as twenty layers of wallpaper have been discovered, revealing an irreplaceable visual history of English printing and design.

Willow Bough, LEFT *and* RIGHT, *one of William Morris's most popular designs.*

A *fine block print of carnations on a dark green ground,* FAR RIGHT, *dating from 1905 to 1925.*

A **M**ANOR HOUSE

A DAZZLING CAST of characters has been connected with this modest brick house. It was built in the 1400s in a village where Ann Boleyn apparently spent some time. King Henry VIII, who fell in love with the beauteous Ann and ultimately made her his second wife, is said to have slept here—no doubt on one of his amorous visits.

By the 18th century, the house belonged to the local lords of the Abingdon family. The sister of the Fourth Earl of Abingdon married Giovanni Gallini, King George III's dancing master, and the Earl gave her this house as a wedding gift. The marriage was not a success, but Signor Gallini cleverly succeeded in keeping the house without the wife. Freed from marital strife and aided by the Italian's royal and artistic patronage, the house became a center for music and art, with Johann Christian Bach and Sir Thomas Gainsborough among the glamorous visitors.

Topiary standing guard in the driveway, PREVIOUS PAGE, sets an intriguing mood for the visitor. Inside the house, an abundance of artistic and musical pleasures—such as the piano in the entrance hall, produced by the same 18th-century craftsman who worked for J. C. Bach. Above it are architectural paintings done by the present owner.

The front of the house, BELOW, as it was when presented to the Fourth Earl of Abingdon's sister in the mid-18th century.

In the entrance hall, RIGHT, a Georgian mahogany bookcase with a glass front lines one wall and a Palladian arch leads to the staircase. Against the left wall is the piano whose detail may be seen on page 247.

"And country life I praise, / And lead, because I find / The philosophic mind / Can take no middle ways." Robert Bridges' lines fit well with his erstwhile house, BELOW. Blocked-up windows on the south wall originate from the days of the Georgian window tax. A detail, LEFT, shows the interestingly asymmetrical window arrangement.

The drawing room, enriched by red silk-covered walls, enhances a collection of family portraits. Sun streams in through the heavy silk curtains, swags held in place by gold feather clips.

Sustaining this creative atmosphere into the next century, the Victorian poet Robert Bridges lived here for 17 years, and died in 1930. The present owner, also an artist and musician, is perpetuating a tradition peculiar to this house, one that has been astonishingly long-lasting even for a country where traditions flourish.

The front facade shows the earliest architecture. Originally, it was only one room deep, but in the 1750s it was rebuilt by Gallini, who added a large ground floor extension at the back, including rooms for dining and dancing lessons. The most recent changes were made by Alfred Waterhouse, the 19th-century architect best known for his Gothic buildings. He made a square roof line, above Gallini's extension, in the Georgian style, thus making the house a perfect cube. The garden was also given a facelift in modern times by landscapist Lanning Roper. The present owners have filled the house with pictures and musical instruments. No house could have been better served by its masters.

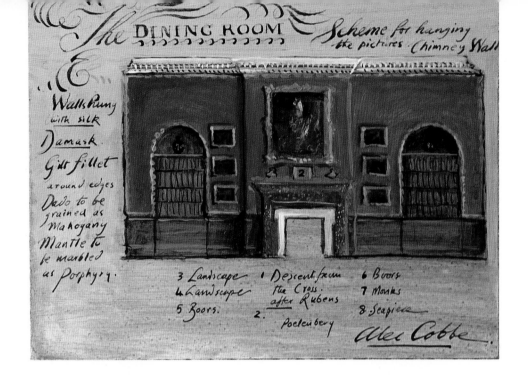

The red color scheme is continued in the dining room, LEFT, *one of the rooms added on by Giovanni Gallini. The purplish black mantel is faux porphyry, another of the owner/ artist's achievements.*

From the extensive collection of musical instruments, BELOW, *a French piano that was made for Marie Antoinette.*

The owner painted a design scheme, ABOVE, *for the hanging of pictures in the dining room.*

The impressive bookcase, BELOW, *is also faux. It is actually a door that leads to another part of the house. (A hinge is visible above the skirting board.)*

*The yellow library is decorated both with family portraits
and some elegant trompe l'oeil vases of flowers painted by the owner.
Behind the painted doors there are bookshelves on
each side of the mantel. Note the dolls' house on the left, made
by the owner. A detail of the mantel,* RIGHT, *with
marble busts and 18th-century vases.*

The upstairs landing, ABOVE, where a Regency-style bookcase is framed by a collection of miniatures.

A *four-poster bed with chintz hangings*, FAR RIGHT, *dominates the master bedroom. A well-used Regency desk is placed between the two windows. The curtains,* RIGHT, *came from Cliveden, the house that once belonged to Nancy Astor. Nancy Lancaster was Lady Astor's niece, and stayed at Cliveden many times, there forming her first ideas about English country house decorating.*

An *English adaptation, in wicker, of a French chaise percée,* BELOW. *Above it, a pretty Regency-style metal bathroom cabinet.*

*Still life, with gulls' eggs,
lunch in the shade of a huge
mulberry tree, the table
encircling its trunk.*

The garden borders, ABOVE LEFT, were designed by the early-20th-century landscape gardener Lanning Roper. He laid out a small incline, with lawn paths dividing a series of flower beds. Fine trees, including a cherry tree, arising from a bed of blue-bells, ABOVE RIGHT, and a copper beech, BELOW RIGHT, punctuate the landscape design. One pathway ends at a stone archway over a small pool, and above it a splendid, currently uninhabited, Victorian birdcage, BELOW LEFT.

*Seats, paths, and lawn provide different aspects of this interesting garden.
An unusually long curved wooden garden seat,* BELOW LEFT, *is a striking
feature, as is the brick path lined with a planting of daffodils,* BELOW RIGHT.

IN SANGVINE VITA ✠ MORIENS CANO

AN ARTIST'S DOLLS' HOUSE

IN A CORNER of the library of the house with a musical past is found the owner's private masterpiece—a dolls' house he made for his daughter. Sternly classical, its exterior is a Georgian fantasy in miniature, crowned with a family motto in Latin. Inside, a masterpiece of miniature artistry is displayed. Every architectural detail is meticulously rendered, every item of furniture at its period best. The floors are divided by central, oval-shaped landings of unsurpassed elegance. Reflecting the owner's own interests, the doll-sized rooms are clearly the home of an artist and musician, whose taste in interior decoration was surely inspired by that of the big house surrounding him.

The front of the dolls' house, showing arrangement of rooms, fine staircase, hall, and balustrade, and handsome pediment. With doors closed, ABOVE, *the dolls' house shows its Georgian lineage.*

263

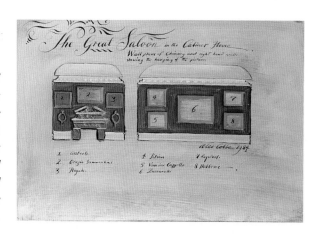

The artist/musician/house builder in his studio, BELOW. *The paneling came from another house, built by the same Alfred Waterhouse who squared the rectangular shape of this manor house.*

The picture-hanging scheme for the great saloon, LEFT — *an example of the designer's perfectionism, even in miniature.*

264

The great saloon complete with family portraits, mantel with broken pediment, and carved ceiling.

The dining room, ABOVE, with wood-paneled walls, a huge romantic landscape painting over the fireplace, brass sconces, and pewter serving dishes.

Signor Gallini himself might have felt at home in this music room, with miniature Royal Doulton china decorating the shelves, ABOVE. The artist's studio, LEFT, with blank canvas. Also at hand are toiletries, a commode, and a fine Chippendale-style chest of drawers.

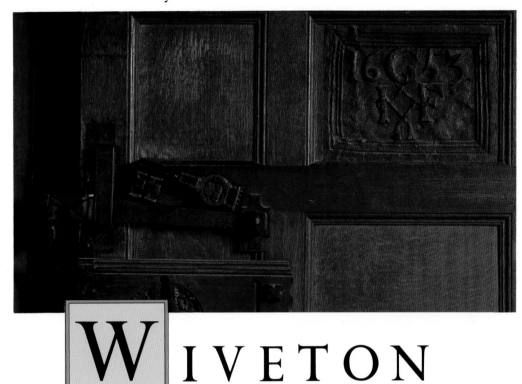

WIVETON

THE HISTORY OF this house is as romantic as its appearance. Its site originally housed a Carmelite priory that was destroyed during the wholesale demolition of the monasteries ordered by Henry VIII in 1538 after the split from Rome. Thanks to the dissolution of these monuments to Catholicism, large tracts of highly desirable English land came on the market for the first time since the Norman Conquest. That is why one finds so many fine houses built on religious foundations.

Situated in a prime position on the coast of East Anglia, with the sea originally reaching right up to the house, the land became an attractive proposition for the overseas traders beginning to prosper in that part of the country in the 17th century. The present house was built in fine style in 1652 and lived in by local merchants for at least a century. The knapped-flint (broken into small

pieces) walls and red brick quoins are typical of local architecture of the period. (The stone-quoined wing was added in 1905–1908.) Floods and wild weather have taken their toll, but its sturdy construction, decorative pediments, and brickwork, surrounding a fine sunken garden, remain one of the most glorious testimonials to that very English combination of common sense and elegance.

The interior of the house reflects its changing fortunes. Described as "the most rambling, inconvenient house imaginable," it was declared before a recent rating evaluation board to be "a housewife's nightmare—over 60 doors, endless steps, no draft-proofing or insulation." That may be, but the rooms have a spaciousness and understated grace that have nothing to do with rate assessments. The big drawing room, part of the Victorian addition by the architect Sir Guy Dawber, is 50 feet long, and originally opened into a billiard room. The beams and moldings were also added by the architect. (Some of these moldings had to be removed by the present owners in order to install the portrait of the ancestor above the fireplace—a naval captain actually, but affectionately known as the Admiral.)

The current owners have also made their mark in other ways. A daughter, Mary MacCarthy, is a distinguished stenciler and a son is a collector and maker of tents. His favorite tent—bought at auction from Gunton Hall, Norfolk—is installed in his bedroom.

The architecture of the old wing of the house, PREVIOUS PAGE, *with its Dutch-style gables, ornate and colorful brickwork, and grand chimneys, was carefully adapted in the new wing on the left by the 20th-century architect Sir Guy Dawber. Fine topiary trees stand guard over the sunken garden, which is interlaced with paths and steps. Close the door and inspect the date—1653. The initials I.G.F. are presumably those of the first owner.*

On the other side of the 1653 door, FAR LEFT, *is a carved stone entrance.*

Pedimented windows, LEFT, *indicate the more recent architecture of the added wing, seen across a meadow of Queen Anne's lace, known more familiarly in England as cow parsley.*

From inside, RIGHT, *a view of the sunken garden.*

The decoration of this room is unnervingly simple—no chintz or other
patterns disrupt the harmony of line and color. Bookcases conceal the much wider opening
formerly made by double doors into the billiard room beyond. To the right
of the opening is the kind of furniture only a room like this could take—a massive
18th-century Italian cabinet inlaid with ivory and mother-of-pearl. "The Admiral"
over the fireplace is an ancestor. The billiard room, with its double-framed
fireplace and classical moldings, is now the dining room.

In this corner of the drawing room, LEFT, the kilim rug on
the floor and rug-covered chaise give warmth and solidity
to what might have been a somewhat chilly space.

This unexceptional chimney
has been beautifully stenciled
by the owners' daughter, Mary
MacCarthy. Family pictures
adorn the walls on each side of
the main stencil design, and
again, plain-colored slipcovers
enhance the decorative effect
of the wall painting.

272

No ordinary bedroom for the stenciler's brother. No ordinary tent, either. Egyptian, quilted, a Durbar tent, it once belonged to a crony of Edward, Prince of Wales, presented during the latter's state visit to India in the mid-1870s.

In these views of the house
and garden, clematis, iris,
geraniums, herbs, and shrubs
make borders for the brick path
leading to the greenhouses.
Another brick path cuts
through the center of the
kitchen garden.

There was once a flint wall
to this garden, which was
destroyed by a flood in 1952.
It was said to have been part
of a compound built to hold
prisoners from two galleons
belonging to the Spanish
Armada. A mulberry tree still
standing in the garden dates
from that time.

The greenhouse, OVERLEAF,
makes a perfect garden room
for entertaining. A striped
cloth, unmatched wicker chairs,
plants all around—the epitome
of summer comfort.

DIRECTORY

This directory lists shops throughout England where you can obtain furniture, fabrics, ceramics and other decorative items featured in the book. Further information can be found in *The British Art & Antiques Directory,* published by The Antique Collector, National Magazine House, 72 Broadwick Street, London W1V 2BP, tel: 01-439 7144. The auction houses, Sotheby's and Christie's, also hold regular sales. Tel: 01-493 8080 and 01-581 2231, respectively.

English country style can be grand or simple; antique shops included here stock large oak kitchen tables, as well as fine 18thC Regency furniture.

Whether you own a country home or not, the directory provides a good guide for where to buy appropriate furnishings, features and fixtures, antique and modern, and a list of interior designers/specialists able to help you create and maintain an English country style.

The listings are accurate on going to press, but of course details may change, so wherever possible please check before acting on the information provided.

INTERIOR DESIGNERS

Designers in Britain tend to undertake a wide range of work and not to specialize in any one look/style. Listed here are those who have experience in domestic interiors. For further information contact the Interior Decorators & Designers Association (IDDA), 45 Sheen Lane, London SW14 8AB, tel: 01-876 4415/6.

Other useful sources are SIAD (Society of Industrial Artists & Designers), 12 Carlton House Terrace, London SW1, tel: 01-930 1911/839 4453; and *Interior Designers Handbook,* published by Grosvenor Press, 50 Grosvenor Street, London W1X 9FH, tel: 01-274 5678.

London

ALAN CHARLES BATE
Scarisbrick & Bate Ltd
111 Mount Street
London W1Y 5HE
Tel: 499 2043
Mostly specializes in traditional work, with a strong emphasis on conservation and restoration of historic houses

NINA CAMPBELL
9 Walton Street
London SW3 2JD
Tel: 225 1011
Specializes in traditional interiors

JANE CHURCHILL LTD
137 Sloane Street, London SW1
Tel: 824 8484
21 Market Place, Kingston-upon-Thames, Surrey
Tel: 549 6292
13 Old Bond Street, Bath, Avon
Tel: 0225 66661

COLEFAX & FOWLER
39 Brook Street, London W1
Tel: 493 2231

DESIGNERS GUILD
271 & 277 King's Road
London SW3
Tel: 351 5775
Well known for its collection of soft furnishings, it also offers an interior design service

FOX LINTON ASSOCIATES
249 Fulham Road, London SW3
Tel: 351 8273

Experienced team of international designers specializing in luxury residential properties

DAVID HICKS
David Hicks Marketing International Ltd
101 Jermyn Street
London SW1
Tel: 627 4400
Well established. His work can be seen in many of the finer private residences in this country and abroad

DAVID LAWS DESIGNS LTD
1/9 Savile Row, London W1
Tel: 437 8487/8412

ANTHONY PAINE
24 Highgate High Street,
Highgate Village
London N6 5JG
Tel: 340 4187
Specializes in the architecture, interior design and decoration of 18th, 19th and early 20thC buildings, designing alterations, additions, specialist joinery and interiors for residential use

Regions

CAROLINE BALER BIRKBECK
The Old Rectory, Shotesham All Saints, Norwich
Norfolk NR15 1YL
Tel: 0508 50362
She undertakes commissions in both modern and traditional style and specializes in private houses both in London and the country

ROSEMARY CANNEY
Rosemary Hearn Interior Design
Westwell, Ashford, Kent
TN25 4JP
Tel: 0233 27682
Specializes in period country houses

JOYCE PATRICIA HUGHES-
FREELAND
Leitch Freeland Ltd
7 Whielden Street
Old Amersham
Buckinghamshire HP7 OJS
Tel: 02403 6296
Her work is mainly concerned with country houses

JULIET JOWITT
The Wood House
Thorpe Lodge
Littlethorpe, Ripon
Yorks HG4 3LU
Tel: 0765 700221
Specializes in country houses – interested in the total look

CAROL R. M. MACMILLAN
Interior Decorations
Altyre House, Gt Horkesley
Colchester
Tel: 0206 271225
Specialist in the country-house field with traditional interiors

JACQUELINE TATE
Hafod Fabrics Ltd
Hillside House
Llanwarne, Herefordshire
Tel: 0981 540367
Specializes in the decoration of English country houses

FABRICS AND WALLPAPERS

For further information and outlets contact The West End Furnishing Fabrics Association, 25 Beford Row, London WC1R 4HN, tel: 01-242 6171, or at 164 Armada Way, Plymouth, tel: 0752 260897.

London

LAURA ASHLEY
183 Sloane Street
London SW1X 9QP
Tel: 235 9728
157 Fulham Road, London SW3
Tel: 584 6939
35 Bow Street, London WC2
Tel: 240 1997
208 Regent Street, London W1
Tel: 734 5824
A catalogue sells in newsagents, listing all branches nationwide. Coordinating floral, geometric, striped and plain cottons, chintzes, wallpaper, bedlinens

BENNISON FABRICS LTD
91 Pimlico Road, London SW1
Tel: 730 3370/8076
Own range of fabrics, 17th-19thC furniture, porcelain, needlework

NINA CAMPBELL
9 Walton Street
London SW3 2JD
Tel: 225 1011
Own range of wallpapers and fabrics, including chintz

JANE CHURCHILL
137 Sloane Street, London SW1
Tel: 824 8484
Own collection inspired by the English country house

COLEFAX & FOWLER CHINTZ SHOP
149 Ebury Street
London SW1W 9QN
Tel: 730 2173
Chintz, cotton, voile and wallpaper based on 18th and 19thC designs

COLLIER CAMPBELL LTD
41 Old Town, London SW4
Tel: 720 7862
Produces furnishing fabrics, dress fabrics and bedlinens, as well as associated products for the English and overseas markets. Over the past 20 years has built up an international reputation for textile design of both originality and creativity

DESIGNERS GUILD
277 King's Road
London SW3 5EN
Tel: 370 5001
Country designs in cottons, wallpapers, curtains and tablecloths, and hand-painted silks

HAMILTON-WESTON WALLPAPERS
10 Lifford Street
London SW15 1NY
Tel: 789 3297
Hand-printed wallpapers in reproduction 19thC designs

CHARLES HAMMOND LTD
165 Sloane Street
London SW1X 9QE
Tel: 235 2151
Country-house chintzes and imported silks, silk-velvets and hand-woven fabrics

HILL & KNOWLES LTD
133 Kew Road, Richmond
Surrey
Tel: 948 4010

LIBERTY & CO
210-220 Regent Street
London W1 6AH
Tel: 734 1234
Liberty's Print Shop
340a King's Road
London SW3 5UR
Tel: 352 6581
Liberty floral prints on lawn cotton, Art Nouveau and William Morris designs, and Collier Campbell

LUNN ANTIQUES
86 New King's Road
London SW6 4LU
Tel: 736 4638
Antique textiles, lacework, embroidery, linens, costume

NATIONAL TRUST SHOP
Blewcoat School
23 Caxton Street
London SW1H OPY
Tel: 222 2877
*And shops throughout the country.
Reproduction late 18th and early
19thC chintzes by David Mlinaric,
based on designs in English stately
homes*

OSBORNE & LITTLE
304 King's Road
London SW3 5UH
Tel: 352 1456
*Own designs in wallcoverings and
fabrics. Retail nationwide*

ARTHUR SANDERSON & SONS LTD
Sanderson House
Berners Street
London W1P 3AD
Tel: 636 7800
*Coordinating fabrics and wallpapers,
including textured, plain, Oriental
and traditional floral designs, and a
range of hand-printed wallpapers*

WARNER & SONS LTD
7-11 Noel Street
London W1V 4AL
Tel: 439 2411
*Reproduction historical furnishing
fabrics and wallpapers*

Regions

G. P. & J. BAKER
West End Road
High Wycombe
Buckinghamshire HP11 2QD

Tel: 0494 33422
London showroom –
18 Berners Street
London W1P 4JA
Quality linens, cottons, wallpapers

BURNS & GRAHAM
4 St Thomas Street, Winchester
Hampshire
Tel: 0962 53779
*Fabrics and furnishings; good-quality
18th and 19thC furniture; brass,
copper; upholstery*

GOLDEN CAGE
99 Derby Road, Canning Circus
Nottingham, Nottinghamshire
Tel: 0602 411600
Linen and lace

THE HONITON LACE SHOP
44 High Street, Honiton, Devon
Tel: 0404 2416
*Antique lace, linens, needleworks and
rugs*

MONKWELL
10-12 Wharfdale Road
Bournemouth, Dorset
Tel: 0202 762456
Furnishing fabrics

TODAY INTERIORS LTD
Hollis Road, Grantham
Lincolnshire NG31 7QH
Tel: 0476 74401
London showroom –
146 New Cavendish Street
London W1M 7FG
Tel: 01-636 0541

ANTIQUES

The following list is intended as a guide to dealers specializing
in English period furniture and *objets d'art*.

London

THE ANTIQUE TRADER
36 & 375 Upper Street
London N1
Tel: 395 2019
English country and period furniture

ASPREY & CO
165-169 New Bond Street
London W1Y OAR
Tel: 493 6767
*Silver, glass, clocks, miniatures,
furniture and objets d'art*

H. BLAIRMAN & SONS LTD
119 Mount Street, London W1
Tel: 493 0444
*18thC English furniture, Regency
furniture*

I. & J. L. BROWN
636 King's Road
London SW6 2DU
Tel: 736 4141
58 Commercial Road
Hereford HR1 2BP
Tel: 0432 58895
*Specializing in English country
furniture*

TONY BUNZL & ZAR DAVAR
344 King's Road, London SW3
Tel: 352 3697
*Good stock of 17th and 18thC
English oak furniture. Also pottery,
brass and objets d'art*

COEXISTENCE LTD
Hobhouse Court
13 Whitcomb Street
London WC2H 7HA
Tel: 839 6620
17 Canonbury Lane,
London N1 2AS
Tel: 226 8382
Country textiles

SIMON COLEMAN
40 White Hart Lane, Barnes
London SW13
Tel: 878 5037
*Country furniture in oak, fruitwood
and pine. English farm tables always
in stock*

THE DINING ROOM SHOP
64 White Hart Lane, Barnes
London SW13 OPZ
Tel: 878 1020
*All kinds of antique furniture for the
dining room, chairs, tables, etc.
Antique porcelain and pottery for the
table, antique glass and decanters,
silver, table linen and lace accessories.
Operates a finding service for
customers*

GENERAL TRADING COMPANY
144 Sloane Street
London SW1X 9BL
Tel: 730 0411
*Antique and reproduction furniture,
objects, porcelain and pewter*

GRAY'S ANTIQUE MARKET
58 Davies Street
London W1Y 1LB
Tel: 629 7034
*Antiques market for small objects
including silver, porcelain and clocks*

GUINEVERE ANTIQUES LTD
578 King's Road, London SW6
Tel: 736 2917
*Large showrooms of antique and
decorative furniture, fine objects and
accessories*

HOTSPUR LTD
14 Lowndes Street
London SW1X 9EX
Tel: 235 1918
*18thC English furniture and
decorative objects*

THE LACQUER CHEST
75 Kensington Church Street
London W8 4BG
Tel: 937 1306
*19thC country and other furniture,
textiles, china, lamps and unusual
objects*

MICHAEL LIPITCH
98 Fulham Road, London SW3
Tel: 589 7327
*Fine quality English 18thC furniture
and decorations, specializing in pairs,
tables, chairs and cabinets*

RELIC ANTIQUES
1 Camden Walk, London N1
Tel: 359 6755
248 Camden High Street, NW1

Tel: 485 8072
and Malmesbury, Wiltshire
*Specialists in decorators' and
collectors' items, architectural
antiques, English country pieces and
garden items*

TOBIAS AND THE ANGEL
68 White Hart Lane, Barnes
London SW13
Tel: 878 8902
*Country furniture, textiles including
bedlinen, especially north country
quilts, tablecloths, pottery, country
objects, kitchen antiques*

ROBERT YOUNG ANTIQUES
68 Battersea Bridge Road
London SW11
Tel: 228 7847
*Antique oak and country furniture,
treen, English folk art and objects*

Regions

ARTHUR BRETT & SONS LTD
40-44 St Giles Street
Norwich, Norfolk NR2 1LW
Tel: 0603 628171
*18thC English furniture. Also
restoration and reproduction*

BROCANTEUSE GALLERY
11 North Street, Ashburton
Devon
Tel: 0364 53389
*Period painted furniture, oak,
primitives, needlework, metalware,
country, decorative objects, early pine*

CLOSE ANTIQUES
19 Little Minster Street
Winchester, Hampshire
SO23 9HA
Tel: 0962 64763
*17th and 18C country furniture,
English pottery, samplers, tiles, early
metal, treen*

COUNTRY INTERIORS
12 Frome Road
Bradford-on-Avon
Wiltshire BA15 1LE
Tel: 02216 4000
*Old country furniture, specializing in
kitchen dressers, locally made oak
furniture, antiquarian prints*

EASTGATE ANTIQUE CENTRE
Black Horse Chambers
6 Eastgate, Lincoln, Lincolnshire
Tel: 0522 44404
*Good-quality period furniture,
watercolour paintings, silver,
jewellery, porcelain, brass, copper,
instruments, clocks and quality
collectors' items*

RUPERT GENTLE ANTIQUES
The Manor House
Milton Lilbourne, Pewsey
Wiltshire SN9 5LQ
Tel: 0672 63344
*18thC English furniture, 16th-
18thC brass, steel and ironwork.
17th and 18thC needlework.
Domestic accessories of the period*

GLOUCESTER HOUSE ANTIQUES
Market Place, Fairford
Gloucestershire GL7 4AB

Tel: 0285 712790
*English country furniture, pottery
and decorative items*

IAN G. HASTIE
46 St Ann Street, Salisbury
Wiltshire SP1 2DX
Tel: 0722 22957
*Large general stock with much 17th,
18th and early 19thC English
antique furniture. Also silver, clocks
and other items*

JOHN NICHOLLS ANTIQUES
27 Long Street, Tetbury
Gloucestershire
Tel: 0666 52781
*Good 17th and 18thC oak and
country furniture, also
complementary items*

**WINDSOR HOUSE ANTIQUES
(LEEDS) LTD**
18/20 Benson Street, Leeds
W. Yorkshire LS7 1BL
Tel: 0943 444666
*18th and 19thC furniture,
metalware, silver and plate,
porcelain, Staffordshire pottery,
clocks and oil lamps*

STANLEY WOOLSTON
29 Broad Street, Ludlow
Shropshire SY8 1NJ
Tel: 0584 3554
*Good antique furniture from 17th,
18th and 19thC and accessories. Also
a gallery of modern fabrics, interior
decoration and design*

POTTERY (MAINLY STAFFORDSHIRE)

London

D. M. & P. MANHEIM
69 Upper Berkeley Street
Portman Square
London W1H 7DH
Tel: 723 6595
*English porcelain, pottery and
enamels 1680-1840*

JEAN SEWELL
3 Campden Street
London W8 7EP
Tel: 727 3122
*18th and 19thC British porcelain
and pottery*

OLIVER-SUTTON ANTIQUES
34c Kensington Church Street
London W8
Tel: 937 0633
*Large collection of Staffordshire
portrait figures*

CONSTANCE STOBO
31 Holland Street
London W8 4LX
Tel: 937 6282
*English lustreware, Staffordshire
animals*

Regions

Stoke-on-Trent is the centre for Staffordshire pottery. Go to
The City Museum and Art Gallery at Hanley
(tel: 0782 273173) for its history.

BRATTON ANTIQUES
Market Place, Westbury
Wiltshire BA13 3DE
Tel: 0373 823021
*English pottery, particularly
Staffordshire; rural and domestic
treen and metalware; mahogany and
country furniture*

GATE ANTIQUES
29 St Saviour's Gate
York, N. Yorkshire YO1 2NQ

Tel: 0904 27035
*Names Staffordshire figures, brass,
copper, glass, Victorian and Georgian
furniture*

WESTON ANTIQUE GALLERY
Boat Lane, Weston, Stafford
Staffordshire ST18 OHU
Tel: 0889 270450
*Staffordshire pottery and porcelain,
maps, prints, glass, silver*

ROCKING HORSES

CLIVE GREEN
The Lychgate
20 Broadmark Lane
Rustington, West Sussex
BN16 2HJ
Tel: 0903 786639
*Maker and restorer of carved wooden
rocking horses*

JOHN RYE
Unit 9
Blake House Farm, Great Sailing

Near Braintree, Essex
Tel: 0371 2548
*Handcarved wooden rocking horses to
traditional designs*

MARGARET SPENCER
Chard Road
Crewkerne, Somerset
TA18 8BA
Tel: 0460 72362
*Handcarved traditional styles;
restoration of antique rocking horses*

DOLLS' HOUSES

London

KAY DESMONDE ANTIQUES LTD
17 Kensington Church Walk
London W8 4NB
Tel: 937 2602
*Antique dolls, dolls' houses, dolls'
house furniture and accessories, toys.
All antique, no reproductions stocked*

THE DOLLS HOUSE TOYS LTD
29 The Market, Covent Garden
London WC2E 8RE
Tel: 379 7243
*Dolls' houses and handmade
miniature furniture*

THE SINGING TREE
69 New King's Road
London SW6
Tel: 736 4527

POLLOCKS TOY MUSEUM
1 Scala Street
London W1
Tel: 636 3452

Regions

LILIAN MIDDLETON'S ANTIQUE
DOLL SHOP
Days Stables, Sheep Street
Stow-on-the-Wold
Gloucestershire GL54 1AA
Tel: 0451 30381
*Antique dolls, dresses and accessories,
dolls' houses and miniatures; antique
doll collection on display. Antique
doll repairs and restoration*

WATERCOLOURS

The following gallery is the home of the Royal Society of Painters in Water Colours, offering watercolours and prints for sale throughout the year:

THE BANKSIDE GALLERY
48 Hopton Street, Blackfriars
London SE1
Tel: 928 7521

Other principal dealers in
London

THOMAS AGNEW & SONS
43 Old Bond Street, London W1
Tel: 629 6176

CHRIS BEETLES
5 Ryder Street, London SW1
Tel: 930 8586

BLOND FINE ART
22 Princes Street, London W1
Tel: 437 1230

COLNAGHI & CO
14 Old Bond Street, London W1
Tel: 491 7408

THE FINE ART SOCIETY
148 New Bond Street
London W1
Tel: 629 5116

THE LEGER GALLERY
13 Old Bond Street, London W1
Tel: 629 3538

MICHAEL PARKIN FINE ART
11 Motcomb Street
London SW1
Tel: 235 8144

SPINK & SON
5 King Street, London W1
Tel: 930 7888

ANDREW WYLD
17 Clifford Street, London W1
Tel: 734 5575

Regions

LINCOLN FINE ART
33 The Strait,
Lincoln, Lincolnshire
Tel: 0522 33029
Fine watercolours, including portrait miniatures and drawings

MARLBOROUGH SPORTING
GALLERY & BOOKSHOP
6 Kingbury Street
Marlborough, Wiltshire
Tel: 0672 54074
Specializing in prints and watercolours of British sport and country pastimes

PELTER/SANDS FINE PAINTINGS
19 The Mall, Clifton, Bristol
Avon BS8 4JG
Tel: 0272 741830
18th, 19th and 20thC watercolours, specializing in landscapes

WALKER GALLERIES
6 Montpellier Gardens
Harrogate, N. Yorkshire
Tel: 0677 67933
Also 3 Cale Street, London SW3
19thC English watercolours

COUNTRY CLOTHES

London

BATES HATTERS
21a Jermyn Street
London SW1
Tel: 734 2722

GIDDENS OF LONDON LTD
15d Clifford Street, London W1
Tel: 734 2788
Saddlery and riding wear

HACKETT GENTLEMANS
CLOTHIERS
65c New King's Road
London SW6
Tel: 731 2790/7129

HARRODS COUNTRY SHOP
Knightsbridge
London SW1X 7XI
Tel: 730 1234

HARVEY NICHOLS
109-205 Knightsbridge
London SW1X 7RJ
Tel: 235 5000

PARKERS OF LONDON LTD
40 Buckingham Palace Road
London SW1
Tel: 828 1670
Also 23 High Street, Aldershot
Hampshire
Tel: 0252 332247

SWAINE, ADENEY, BRIGG & SONS LTD
185 Piccadilly, London W1
Tel: 734 4277

Regions

J. BARBOUR & SONS
Simonside, South Shields
Tyne & Wear
Tel: 0632 55251

BOOTS & SADDLES
14 Bishopric
Horsham, Sussex
Tel: 0403 69441

HUSKY OF TOSTOCK
Box 9, Bury Street
Stowmarket, Suffolk
Tel: 0449 674471/4

ARCHITECTURAL ARTEFACTS

The following comprises a list of places where you can acquire structural features and fixtures, such as fireplaces, panelling and brass fittings.

Names of conservator and restorer specialists, in many different fields, including furniture, painting, ceramics and textiles, can be found in *The British Art & Antiques Directory 1987,* published by The Antique Collector, National Magazine House, 72 Broadwick Street, London W1V 2BP, tel: 01-439 7144.

Useful names and addresses

INTERNATIONAL INSTITUTE FOR CONSERVATION
6 Buckingham Street
London WC2N 6BA
Tel: 839 5975

UNITED KINGDOM INSTITUTE FOR CONSERVATION
Tate Gallery, Millbank
London SW1P 4RG
Tel: 821 1313

MUSEUMS AND GALLERIES COMMISSION
7 St James's Square
London SW1Y 4JU
Tel: 839 9341
(Conservation/restoration of craft objects)

ROYAL INSTITUTE OF BRITISH ARCHITECTS
66 Portland Place, London W1
Tel: 580 5533

London

ACQUISITIONS (FIREPLACES) LTD
269 Camden High Street
London NW1 7BX
Tel: 485 4955
Original and reproduction cast-metal early-Victorian fireplaces, brass grates and fenders, fire irons and coal buckets

ARCHITECTURAL ANTIQUES LTD
133 Upper Street, London N1
Tel: 226 5565
Fireplaces, stained glass, garden furniture, statuary, panelled rooms, wrought iron, large furniture, decorative antiques

J. D. BEARDMORE & CO LTD
3 Percy Street
London W1P 9FA
Tel: 637 7041
Reproduction door and cabinet fittings in brass and black iron

C. P. HART
Newnham Terrace
Hercules Road
London SE1 7DR
Tel: 928 5866
Reproduction Victorian free-standing baths

GEORGE JACKSON
Rathbone Works
Rainville Road
London W6 9HD
Tel: 385 6616
Plaster-moulded reproduction early 17th-late 19thC architectural ornaments, including cornices, centrepieces, panels, plaques and columns. Also reproduction timber fireplaces

KNOBS & KNOCKERS TRADE AND DESIGN
36-40 York Way
London N1 9AB
Tel: 278 8925
One of the UK's most comprehensive stockholdings of architectural ironmongery from period to contemporary

THE LONDON ARCHITECTURAL SALVAGE & SUPPLY CO LTD
The Mark Street Depository
Mark Street, off Paul Street
London EC2A 4ER
Tel: 739 0448
(Also Door Store, King Johns Court, London EC2: repairs and sells period doors)

Specialist suppliers of architectural relics of every description, including doors, panelling, chimney pieces, ironwork, glass

H. W. POULTER & SON
279 Fulham Road
London SW10 9PZ
Tel: 352 7268
Marble chimney pieces, fire grates, brass chandeliers, wood mantelpieces

THORNHILL GALLERIES LTD
76 New King's Road
London SW6
Tel: 736 5830
Marble, stone and wooden chimney pieces. Fire grates and fenders. Architectural features, wood carvings, panelled rooms

Regions

ARCHITECTURAL ANTIQUES
The New Savoy Show Rooms
New Road
South Molton, Devon
Tel: 076 95 3342
(Also "An Englishman's Home" 56 Stokes Croft, Bristol)
Architectural antiques, panelling, fire surrounds, doors, stained & leaded glass, Victorian bathroom fittings

ARCHITECTURAL HERITAGE OF CHELTENHAM
Boddington Manor
Boddington, near Cheltenham
Gloucestershire GL51 0TJ
Tel: 0242 68741

Period architectural fittings, including wood panelling, doors, gates, fireplaces and grates, and garden statuary, fountains and stone seats

CROWTHER OF SYON LODGE
Syon Lodge, Busch Corner
London Road
Isleworth, Middlesex TW7 5BH
Tel: 01-560 7978/7985
Very large and important stock of garden ornaments, chimney pieces, panelled rooms, wrought ironwork and period architectural features

DALESIDE ANTIQUES
St Peter's Square
Cold Bath Road
Harrogate, N. Yorkshire
HG2 0NP
Tel: 0423 60286
Specialists in old and period pine furniture, architectural features & fittings, decorative accessories

DICKENSON AND THOMAS
Old Granary, 10 North Street
Stamford

Lincolnshire PE9 2YN
Tel: 0780 62236
Mainly pine and country furniture and architectural fitments

HALLIDAYS ANTIQUES LTD
The Old Cottage, High Street
Dorchester
Oxfordshire OX9 8HL
Tel: 0865 340028
(Also 28 Beauchamp Place
London SW3)
17th-19thC furniture and paintings; period and reproduction wood and marble fireplaces; period room panelling. All accessories for the period fireplace

ANDY THORNTON
ARCHITECTURAL ANTIQUES LTD
Ainleys Industrial Estate, Elland
W. Yorkshire HX5 9JP
Tel: 0422 78125
Large stocks of architectural antiques, including panelling, doors, etched, cut and stained glass

GARDEN FURNITURE AND STATUARY

London

CLIFTON NURSERIES
5a Clifton Villas
Warwick Avenue
London W9 2PH
Tel: 289 6851
Antique and modern garden furniture and statuary

MALLETT AT BOURDON HOUSE
2 Davies Street
Berkeley Square
London W1Y 1LJ
Tel: 629 2444
Antique garden statuary, ornaments on display in courtyard

Regions

ARCHITECTURAL HERITAGE OF
CHELTENHAM
Boddington Manor
Boddington

Nr Cheltenham, Gloucestershire
Tel: 0242 68741
18th and 19thC figures available from a complete selection of period garden statuary, including antique stone and marble pieces

THE GREAT MALVERN ANTIQUES
ARCADE
Salisbury House, 6 Abbey Road
Malvern, Hereford and
Worcester WR14 3HG
Tel: 06845 5490
Over 2000 sq ft of decorative antiques and garden furniture

HOUSES IN THE BOOK OPEN TO THE PUBLIC

SLEDMERE HOUSE
Driffield, Yorkshire
Open Easter weekend, Bank
holidays, 29 May-30 Sept.
Closed Mondays and Fridays.
Groups by appointment.
Tel: 0377 86208

DODDINGTON HALL
near Lincoln
Open Wednesdays, Sundays and
Bank Holiday Mondays from

May to September. Also Easter
Monday. Groups by
appointment.
Tel: 0522 690980

DEENE PARK
Corby, Northamptonshire
Open Sundays in June, July and
August. Groups by
appointment.
Tel: 078085 78/361

GARDENS IN THE BOOK OPEN TO THE PUBLIC

HERGEST CROFT GARDENS
Kington, Herefordshire
Open daily end of April to mid-
September, and every Sunday
until the last week in October.
Groups by appointment.
Tel: 0544 230160

HEALE HOUSE GARDEN
Middle Woodford, near
Salisbury, Wiltshire

Open Good Friday to end of
September, Monday to
Saturday, and every first Sunday
of the month. Groups by
appointment.
Tel: 072273 207

HELMINGHALL HALL GARDENS
Ipswich, Suffolk
Open Easter Sunday to 30
September, Sundays only.

For a complete listing of houses and gardens in England open
to the public, consult *Historic Houses, Castles and Gardens,* a
comprehensive guide published annually by ABC Historic
Publications, World Timetable Centre, Church Street,
Dunstable, Bedfordshire. Tel: 0582 600111.

BIBLIOGRAPHY

A huge number of books have been written on English country
houses. This list is limited to those readily available and of
interest to the non-specialist reader.

CHAMBERS, JAMES, AND GORE, ALAN. *The English House.* 1985
CLIVE, MARY. *The Day of Reckoning.* 1964
COOK, OLIVE. *The English House Through Seven Centuries.* Photographs by
Edwin Smith. 1983
GIROUARD, MARK. *Life in the English Country House. A Social and Architectural
History.* 1980
MUTHESIUS, STEFAN. *The English Terraced House.* 1982
ROBINSON, JOHN MARTIN. *The Latest Country Houses.* 1984
SCOTT-JAMES, ANN, AND LANCASTER, OSBERT. *The Pleasure Garden.* 1979
WATERSON, MERLIN, ed. *The Country House Remembered: Recollections of Life
Between the Wars.* 1985
YARWOOD, DOREEN. *English Interiors, A Pictorial Guide and Glossary.* 1983

INDEX